D0282575

Raising
PIGS
Successfully

Raising PIGS Successfully

Kathy and Bob Kellogg

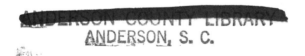
ANDERSON COUNTY LIBRARY
ANDERSON, S. C.

WILLIAMSON PUBLISHING
CHARLOTTE, VERMONT 05445

Copyright © 1985 by Kathy and Bob Kellogg

All rights reserved. No portion of this book may be
reproduced — mechanically, electronically or by any
other means, including photocopying — without written
permission of the publisher.

Library of Congress Cataloging in Publication Data

Kellogg, Kathy.
  Raising pigs successfully.

  Includes index.
  1. Swine. I. Kellogg, Bob. II. Title.
SF395.K38 1985 636.4'0068 85-6542
ISBN 0-913589-15-2

Cover and interior design: Trezzo-Braren Studio
Typography: Villanti & Sons, Printers, Inc.
Printing: Capital City Press
All photographs not otherwise credited are by
Kathy Kellogg.

Williamson Publishing Co.
Box 185
Charlotte, Vermont 05445
800–234–8791

Manufactured in the United States of America

20 19 18 17 16 15 14 13 12 11

Dedication

To our Ms. Piggy and her brood of pampered piglets who taught us more about raising pigs than any book we ever read.

Contents

Acknowledgements

Many people help to make a book like this possible. We would like to recognize some of them:

Special thanks to Jack and Susan Williamson, our publishers, and Andrea Chesman, our editor, for their faith and technical assistance. Gratitude is also extended to Ruth Price, USDA Photography Division; Al Keating, The American Farm Bureau; Mark W. Thomas, Vice President, Pork and Processed Meat, The Pork Industry Group of the Meat Board; Senator Dan Evans; Dave Nichols, Kansas State University; Larry L. Rus, The National Pork Producers Council; The Cooperative Extension Service at Washington State University; and all the county agricultural agents, veterinarians, and neighboring hog farmers who have given us their help and valuable input.

Chapter 1

INTRODUCING PIGS AND PORK PRODUCTION

Congratulations! If you selected this book to read, you are obviously serious about raising your own pork. Maybe you're fed up with high supermarket prices, or you would like to eat more flavorful, tender pork, or you have a few acres to spare and feel pigs could use it. Whoever you are and whatever motivates you, your goal is probably the same as ours: good food that you raised yourself at a bargain price.

Primarily, this book is written for the small, hobby, hog farmers. Raising hogs does not require a lot of money or time; the chores can fit easily around a full-time job. Most small-scale growers raise 1 to 3 pigs a year (generally during the mild spring to fall period) from weaner stage to market weight. This provides plenty of meat for most families, plus an extra hog or two to sell to friends and relatives.

Hogs do quite well on a commercial ration supplemented with home grown garden, dairy, and egg surpluses, as well as nutrients gleaned from pasture and soil. You can hire a professional to butcher your hogs, or you can slaughter and butcher on the farm. Although home-butchered meat cannot be sold or traded and is a great deal of extra work, it may be worth doing just to see if you can.

Very few small-scale pig raisers ever go commercial, but many try farrowing (breeding) a sow for fun (which it can be) or with visions of instant riches (not a realistic expectation). Some hog experts even claim that it is all but impossible to make a living raising hogs on a small-scale today. No matter, pigs are fun, pork is good, and homegrown pork is the best.

In this book, we've relied on our own personal experience in pork production as well as on the experiences and writings of others. We've also included the insights we've gained from our pigs—as well as some of the mistakes we made when we were first starting out (some seem quite humorous, now, but didn't at the time).

The wild boar is ancestor to all the modern domestic swine breeds.

PIGS IN HISTORY

Meat, including pork, has been a primary dietary component of humans since the earliest days of recorded history. Nonetheless, pigs have been the victims of bad press almost from the beginning—right back to the Old Testament and religious prohibitions against the eating of "unclean meat," which included pork. Carry-over swine bigotry surfaces in phrases such as "dirty pig," "filthy as a pigsty," and the 1960s' derogatory nickname for the police. Nonetheless, pigs and pork have their place in human society, despite the negative image they often have to overcome.

Modern domesic swine breeds can all be traced back to the original wild boars of China and Europe, night creatures of the forest with straight tails, dark colors, long snouts, poor eyes, and rough backs (hence, the nickname "razorbacks"). By contrast, the modern hog is a more social night-sleeper with longer intestines (greater feed efficiency) than his wild cousins.

For centuries, hogs have been important to man. First hunted in the forest for meat, hogs have been used to root for truffles in France, harnessed for driving, trained to hunt, used to clear forests, and raised for lard (used in soap, candles, cooking fat), bristles (for brushes), and pigskin leather, which is tough yet soft and spongy. The old chiché that everything is usable except the squeal is not too far from the truth. Today, hogs are responsible for such pharmaceutical and industrial products as insulin, heart valves, skin for burn victims, ball bearings, and hair brushes.

Swine are not native to North America. Legend tells that early explorers brought them on voyages and set them free to roam wild as they had done in Europe. The American climate and environment agreed with these first porkers, and they multiplied rapidly. Early New England colonists continued the traditions of Europe and allowed the hogs to range in nearby woods and pastures. The mature animals were lean, but stringy and tough (rangy). No owners claimed the numerous swine, and at market time, the colonists hunted them individually with dogs. Because the swine averaged only 150 to 200 pounds full-grown, they weren't difficult to catch. Today, mature males can weigh well over 1,000 pounds!

It wasn't long before the early Americans realized that if they kept the hogs penned during the final months of their lives and fed them with corn and other foodstuffs, a plumper porker known as *chuffy* would result. Since lard and tallow were important by-products for soap, candles, and cooking, the practice of penning and fattening hogs had begun.

Today, lean, meat-type hogs have replaced the rangy wild boars and chuffy hogs of the past. Since our need for excess fat has all but disappeared, modern hogs are long, lean, and have more flesh on their sides and quarters than historical hogs. Further, swine today are more efficient feeders, that is they grow faster with less grain. It's not surprising, then, that over one-third of the world's red meat supply is pork.

WHY RAISE YOUR OWN FEEDER HOGS?

Quite honestly, feeder hogs are among the easiest and the cheapest meat animals to raise. Cash outlay is small when compared to other livestock and the feeding period from weaning to butcher is far less than, say, a beef cow. Further, 2 hogs will take care of the average family's pork requirements for an entire year.

What you are looking at is a short-term, low-labor, low-risk commitment when raising feeder hogs for pork. At the longest, they'll be around 5 to 6 months; at the most, your daily labor should average about 15 to 30 minutes a day. Pigs need only warmth in the winter, cool in the summer, proper feed, dry bedding, and fresh water. Further, if given the opportunity, pigs are among the cleanest of all the farm animals, which is a far cry from a widespread belief to the contrary. They will pick a single area for a toilet, easing manure-removal chores, and they will not lay in the filth or move in it if they have a clean place to sleep.

When you raise feeders, you purchase a weaned pig from a breeder and then feed it to market/butcher weight. This is a popular way to go, avoiding the high-labor, high-loss management problems associated with breeding herds and newborns. In fact, 40 percent of all hogs slaughtered are not raised on the farm where they were born.

We recommend that you raise weaner pigs for your pork. You will be in control of what they eat and how they live. Further, you will know how healthy they are at butcher time. Do not purchase an old sow or boar to eliminate the labor and expense of raising the animal yourself. What you save in terms of time and money will never equal what you lose in quality. Although it may seem like you get more meat for your dollar, you do not control age and lifestyle if you buy a mature hog, and this may result in less tender meat, sometimes fit only for sausage.

Many pork producers raise feeders by the thousand. The trend is toward fewer hog producers raising more hogs per farmer. However, management problems associated with large numbers and overcrowding must be solved. Hence, the popular use of antibiotics in feeds to prevent stress-related diseases. As small producers, we don't have to worry about that.

But, beyond the financial and labor considerations, raising feeder pigs is just plain fun. Hogs are intelligent and affectionate and can easily grow into pets if you're not careful. Most love to have their ears scratched and their stomachs rubbed. Many will learn to come when called or when they see a feed bucket passing by their pen. But resist the temptation to become too attached and follow the old homesteader's rule: If you're going to eat it, don't give it a pet name. Try something like "Porky" or "Chops" or "Spareribs" if the urge to name is too strong.

WHY LEARN THE TECHNICAL STUFF?

Most people want to raise only a couple of pigs and wonder how much they need to know about swine production. We think it makes little sense to struggle with the old-fashioned trial-and-error method when you can learn from the mistakes and successes of farmers who make their living producing quality pork. Education can only make you more efficient whether you raise 2 or 200 porkers; ignorance can cost time and money. Read and evaluate all the pork producing information that is available to you before you begin. Then, visit local farmers, butchers, feed stores, and veterinarians to learn even more. Ask questions—find answers. Know the market and understand the laws. Strive to be the most efficient raiser that you can be; top quality meat in your freezer will be your reward.

PORK PRODUCTION OVERVIEW

Start by checking with your county extension agent and zoning clerk to be sure that there are no laws against your pork-production venture. What, you protest, could there actually be laws against pigs? Oh, yes indeed. Zoning regulations vary widely regarding where and how many hogs you can produce. In fact, in some places, old myths about hog quarters being a literal "pigstye" and an eyesore, as well as beliefs that all hog pens stink unbearably, have led many rural developments to ban oinkers. Check your purchase or rental agreements, as well as the state and county zoning laws and local ordinances, before beginning any swine shopping trips or building ventures.

Plan your pork production period for the most easily managed weather: spring through summer. Your hogs will be ready to butcher before winter sets in, which eliminates the need for extensive, heated shelters.

We begin with weaner pigs purchased from a local farmer. Locating reliable sellers isn't difficult; try the classified section of the newspaper, feed stores, custom butchers, or other raisers. Select several potential markets and visit each before making your purchase.

Depending on your location, you may have a large number of breeds to choose from, or your selection, like ours in the Pacific Northwest, may be very limited. We discuss all the major breeds in a later chapter, but we don't recommend that you concern yourself too much with this aspect if you are just beginning. Any well-treated pig should produce quality pork.

An 8-week-old pig, weighing 20 to 35 pounds, could be purchased for $30 to $40 in 1984. At that time, $1 a pound was a fair selling price; anything less was a bargain.

We don't buy piglets younger than 8 weeks of age, although sometimes they sell for a reduced price, because there is a greater disease and early death risk. The producer we buy from will let us select our weaners when they are only 4 to 6 weeks old, but he insists that we leave them on his farm until they are at least 2 months of age.

We select large, active females or castrated males and have noticed no growth rate differences between the sexes. We recommend raising 2 pigs at a time. They appreciate the company and will snuggle up together to sleep. Furthermore, being pigs, they will compete at mealtimes, eating more and growing faster. If that seems like too much pork, consider selling the second hog at or after butcher. Marketing the extra animal will cut down considerably on your expenses, too.

The basic requirements for raising 2 pigs are shelter, fencing, feed, water, your daily labor, and a little love. We'll cover these subjects in depth in the following chapters, but for now you must understand that producing quality pork is more than simply throwing a bucket of slop into the pigpen once in awhile.

The shelter requirement can be satisfied by almost anything from a barn to a shed to a lean-to. Pigs raised only during the warm months of the year don't need elaborate housing since the main goal is to provide shade and protection from wind and rain. We use portable, floorless structures and provide plenty of clean straw for bedding. Our animals have never complained and our shelter costs are practically zero, since we rely on scavanged building materials.

Fencing is a little more complicated with pigs because they are natural diggers. A pig will root (dig with its shovel-like nose) under a fence faster than he will go over or through it. We've used a variety of fences over the years but prefer to combine recycled lumber with electric and/or barbed wire. Although many raisers claim you can get by with just a strand of wire, we feel more secure and the pigs seem to have more respect when they can actually see the fence.

Pigs grow faster than any other farm animal and, with proper feeding, will gain nearly 250 pounds in 6 months.If you feed only a commercial ration, expect to pay $80 to $100 for feed (1984 figures). You can lower your costs by locating a bulk dealer and providing your own containers, which is what we do. Supplementing a commercial diet with garden produce, fruit, eggs, bakery goods, and dairy products can cut your feeding costs by up to 20 percent.

When your hogs have reached butcher weight (225 to 250 pounds), it's time to decide who will process the meat. If you intend to sell part of the pork, plan to have your animals slaughtered in an approved facility under the supervision of a state or USDA meat inspector. The law specifically states that unless you do this, your meat is not approved for sale or trade. Also, if you're a first-timer or you tend to grow attached to the porkers, transporting to a slaughterhouse might be worth the extra money. It's much easier to say goodbye at the truck and only see the meat when it returns ready for your freezer.

If you decide to use a commercial facility, shop around. Rates as well as cleanliness and other factors vary widely.

On the other hand, if you are using your meat strictly for home consumption, you have 2 other options: butcher them yourself or hire a custom farm slaughterer to do the job on the farm.

We usually send our butcher hogs to a slaughterhouse, especially when we intend to market the meat. However, we've had excellent results with farm slaughters done by professionals, too. We have not tried to slaughter our animals and cut the meat ourselves.

And what can you expect to bring to the freezer after all is said and done? On the average, a 225-pound hog will dress out to about 175 pounds of pork, which includes hams, bacon, ribs, roasts, sausage, chops, steaks, liver, heart, kidneys, hocks, head, feet, tongue, tail, and fat—more than enough to satisfy our family of 4 for up to a year.

Probably the best part of raising your own food, whether it be pork or beef or eggs or garden goods, is the satisfaction you receive knowing exactly where that food came from and exactly how it was produced. And, as you will find out with pigs, raising the critters is half the fun!

Whether you raise a thousand hogs with the commercial goal of making a profit or feed a couple for your own pork supply, the key to success is good management. Well-managed poor hogs do better than poorly managed good hogs. The art, skill, and caring you put into finding weaners and then housing and feeding them will determine, in large part, the quality of meat you produce.

Although management is definitely an individual process with no set rules or methods, producing meat efficiently in terms of labor and capital has well-accepted guidelines no matter what the scale of the hog-raising operations. That is what the remainder of this book will explain. Then, beyond the guidelines, you're on your own! Just don't forget to enjoy your porkers because you can't possibly do a good job with something you don't enjoy.

Chapter 2

THE
MODERN
DOMESTIC HOG

Welcome to the world of the hog. And a wide world it is indeed! According to the USDA, over one-third of the world's hogs are in China, with the USA's "Corn Belt" second, and Brazil third. From the Americas to Europe to Asia, hogs can be found contributing food and other important products to the human environment.

The best place to begin as we explore this world is with a few terms. Already we have used such words as "pig," "hog," and "swine" in this book. What do they mean? *Swine* is a generic term for every kind of hog and pig. *Pig* is a word generally confined to swine weighing under 120 pounds, while *hog* refers to those over 120 pounds. However, in Britain, *all* swine are pigs.

A little further, *piglets* are newborn pigs, *weaners* or *shoats* are weaned (naturally) pigs weighing 25 to 40 pounds, *feeders* or *finishers* are pigs from weaning age to market size, and *market hogs*, weighing about 220 pounds, are ready for butcher. *Sows* are older females who have given birth to 1 or more litters of piglets, and *gilts* are younger females usually destined to become mothers. *Boars* are sexually mature males used for breeding. *Barrows* are males that were castrated at a young age and are destined for the production of pork. Boars that are castrated when mature are called *stags*.

You may also encounter terms such as "barbecue (Bar-B-Q) pig," which is a smaller-sized pig, generally under 100 pounds, that is cooked whole. A "SPF hog" (Specific Pathogen Free) is born by caesarean section in a sterile environment. "Mini-pigs" are used in the United States for laboratory work. These animals are 12 inches tall and 18 inches long at maturity. In Europe, they are raised on kitchen scraps to provide pork in a matter of weeks instead of months. Beyond these terms there is a whole host of porcine jargon understood only by producers. If you are interested in learning this foreign language, try the glossary in the back of this book for a starter. Then, go hang around a hog farm for a few hours.

SWINE PHYSIOLOGY

The modern meat hog is not the same animal it was 100 years ago. Our grandfathers had a breeding goal of round, fat, lard-type animals ("chuffy") with short legs and heavy jowls (the portion of a hog's neck between his mouth and his front legs). Then, when lard lost its value as synthetics and vegetable oils took its place, breeders began to concentrate on producing an intermediate type hog somewhere between the leggy, rangy, lean wild boar and the chuffy lard-type. This is the "meat type" animal we have today. Meat hogs have strong legs, meaty shoulders, large hams, and good body length for plenty of lean bacon and chops.

Fat "chuffy" type   Leggy type   Meat type

Hog types.

Commercially, the modern meat hog is graded and valued by the amount of backfat and the total carcass muscling based on the "loin eye area," which is a band of muscle running parallel to the backbone. Loin eye area measurements indicate the amount of prime cuts that can be expected from the carcass. The national standard is 4½ square inches of loin eye area.

Hogs do not marble their fat in the muscle like beef, but rather lay it down in wide bands like you see in bacon. The measurement of fat along the backbone is a good indication of the amount of fat in the entire body. Modern producers use a special probe or ultrasonic device (some even use a simple knife-and-ruler technique) to keep a check on the backfat thickness of their hogs. Ideally, it is no more than 1½ inches thick.

Although commercial raisers use special tools and techniques to measure the loin eye and backfat so that they can estimate the meat quality of their live animals, we don't believe that small-scale raisers need to be concerned with determining these measurements.

Unlike other farm animals, the cardiovascular, digestive, and respiratory systems of hogs are similar to our own. Even our nutritional needs are about the same. In addition, man and swine share similar diseases, such as influenza and pneumonia. For this reason, the pig (especially the mini-pig) is an ideal laboratory animal for the study of human systems. The similarities also make swine raising a little easier to understand: if you could live and prosper with certain foods and housing, chances are your hogs could live and prosper with it, too.

PARTS OF THE PIG

Let's take a closer look at the marvelous pork-producing machine. We'll start at that unique nose, called a *snout* in the pig trade. A pig's nose is designed for 2 things: digging and scent detection. It ends in a floating disc of cartilage tied to muscle that can be moved about in the soil like a shovel. If you've ever watched a rooting pig at work, you know how powerful that snout can be. Rocks, tree roots, even fencelines are no obstacle for the hog.

The other use of the nose is scent detection. Pigs have poor eyesight, possibly a carry-over from their night-roaming wild days. However, their senses of smell and taste are intensified to make up for what they lack visually. When a hog investigates something strange, chances are he will do it by sniffing it, rooting at it, and nibbling on it.

Another interesting hog feature is at the other end, the tail. Unless it is cut off (docked) early in life to prevent other pigs from biting it off, the hog has a unique curled up end-piece. Most hog producers will tell you that you can tell exactly how a hog feels by looking at his tail. A highly curled, upward tail is a sure sign of a healthy, happy hog.

Most raisers will routinely dock their animals' tails if many will be housed together in limited space. Since we raise only 2 or 3 animals at a time, we've never experienced tail-biting with our pigs. Personally, we like curly pig tails and would rather ours have theirs intact.

Yes, hogs have sharp teeth and, yes, they have been known to bite. Little piglets nibbling on your pants leg with affection and play in mind may be cute and innocent enough. However, a 1,000-pound boar or a sow with a litter, or even a full-grown 220-pound market hog, is a potentially dangerous animal.

The unique pig snout was made for digging!

Some raisers claim that you can break a pig of a biting habit with a sharp slap on the snout. Other hog farmers say that such discipline measures often backfire and produce a more aggressive animal.

We raise our pigs about the same way that we raise our dogs. Aggressive behavior is dealt with immediately and punishment begins when the animals are still young and small enough to be intimidated by a large human. Further, punishment is delivered every time the unwanted behavior, such as biting, occurs. We've had success by slapping the animal on the snout with a hand or a stick (we prefer a stick because the animal will then associate the punishment with the tool, not our hands) accompanied by the loud, firm command, "NO!" Eventually, if we even pick up a stick or yell the "NO!" command, the animal will cease misbehaving without needing the slap.

Luckily, well-cared-for swine rarely attack a human. However many will bite on legs, shoes, hands, and anything else within reach just because they enjoy nibbling. Wear the proper clothing around hogs. We've found that long sleeves, long pants, and waterproof boots are essential for protection. The few times we tried feeding our pigs wearing shorts or sandals, we ended up either very dirty or nibbled almost to pain or both!

Although older children can and often do become friends with the porkers, don't let small children in or near the pen unattended. The potential for injury is just too great to take any chances. However, children beyond the age of 8 or 9 can help with chores if you teach them early to respect the hogs. We've found that our children tire of them when the pigs grow out of babyhood. After 100 pounds, they get too big to cuddle. Also, because meat hogs are only on the farm for a very short time, children are not likely to adopt them as pets.

PIG TALK

Another lesser-known hog fact: pigs talk. There's the shrieking squeal of fear, the "bark" or "woof" of alarm or warning, the anguished roars of hungry pigs, and the satisfied grunts of happy hogs. But the best of the swine language is the happy talk of a sow nursing her litter.

We've found that with a little time spent communicating in the pigpen, most hogs will respond to the human voice. Many of ours have learned to "talk" to us with breathy "oof-oof-oof" sounds. We've even had a few "kissing pigs" who took communication a step further—just one of the many joys of hog raising!

PIG BEHAVIOR

Under natural conditions, hogs have natural tendencies. Modern confinement housing has eliminated most of these. However, if you, like most small-scale raisers, intend to keep your animals in open, outdoor pens or on pasture, you will notice some common behaviors. As mentioned earlier, pigs tend to define a toilet area and deposit feces away from their sleeping quarters. Also, they will root and dig in any earth available for tasty edibles such as earthworms, grubs, and roots. If the land available has pasture grasses growing on it, the pigs will graze on it—although the urge to root will probably predominate eventually.

Another common behavior is wallowing in water or mud in hot weather. Hogs are extremely sensitive to heat and can suffer from sunburn and heat stroke just like humans. Wallowing not only prevents these occurrences but also helps control skin parasites. We've found that if there is any way for a hog to tip over a watering trough and create a wallow, he will do it.

All pigs enjoy a good scratch!

Wallowing in the mud is a typical hog behavior.

Pigs like to scratch and be scratched. In some cases, it is an intense need caused by insects and skin disease. But mostly, hogs will rub against fencing, housing, and anything else handy just because they enjoy a good scratch. We've had spoiled pigs that would rub against our legs and demand that we accommodate their scratching desires—immediately.

Probably more than any other farm animal, pigs like to play. They'll run in circles and chase each other, barking and grunting in delight. Also, pigs like "toys," which can be anything from a forgotten feed bucket to an old cardboard box or feed sack.

At the University of Illinois, a research team found that strips of cloth tied to a fence were the most popular pig toys; hogs played with them for a week or more. Other items such as newspapers, boxes, and plastic garbage cans were also enjoyed, but forgotten more easily. Researchers also discovered that pigs won't play with any toys dirtied by manure.

A pig's interest span isn't very long in any case and they tire of the same toy quickly, but half the fun of raising pigs is watching their antics. Certainly, hogs are far more entertaining than any other meat animal you can raise!

It is possible and probably desirable to raise happy, well-trained, contented pigs on a small-scale. We can't say for sure that the pork is better when the pig is happy, but we believe it could be. In any case, many potential problems (biting, escaping, and stress-related illness to name a few) can be avoided by learning how your hogs function. You can begin to achieve this goal by understanding how a hog's body and mind work. Then, by respecting and taking into consideration parts of a pig's nature such as digging, wallowing, and nibbling, you will be more prepared for the task of raising him. Finally, spend some of your time learning pig talk and watching pig play. If nothing more, it certainly makes the chores more enjoyable.

Chapter 3

SWINE BREEDS
AND
CHARACTERISTICS

The breed of hog you select for pork production is not critical to your success. Any feeder chosen from a well-run hog farm should do well. In fact, 90 percent of the hogs raised in the United States are crossbred (we'll explain why later in this chapter), which is what you will probably decide to raise.

There is no best breed despite the fact that all breeding associations claim their breed tops the list. More important to the pork producer than breed is type: long and lean ("bacon-type") or short and fat ("lard-type"). The type of meat hog available to you, the finisher, is based on consumer demand, which influences what the breeder selects. Modern hog breeds fall somewhere between the lard-type and the very lean, leggy bacon-type. Today's ideal hog, breed aside, is meaty with good body length, heavy bone, no excess backfat, and at least 4 square inches of loin eye. A hog's color, head and face shape, and ear type (characteristics mainly affected by breed) have little to do with meat quality and tend to be personal preferences of breeders and raisers.

FACTORS TO CONSIDER

The best breed for you as a pork producer depends on several factors. The first is availability. Not all breeds are available in all parts of the country. If you live in the Corn Belt, Iowa say, then your choice of breed is virtually unlimited. If, however, you live in the Pacific Northwest like we do, or in some other non-hog-producing area, you take what you can get.

The next factors to consider are growth rate, feed efficiency, and carcass quality (fat versus lean). Your basic goal is to produce lean pork as fast and efficiently as possible. Sometimes breeds differ in their basic growing abilities, but, then again, any well-cared-for feeder hog will probably perform well.

Finally, consider temperament and disease resistance. You want to raise a docile, durable, fast-growing, quality porker with little invested in veterinarians and medications.

You may not care much about hog breeds when you are first starting out or even if you raise your own pork for many years. Eventually, though, you will probably want to know more about this subject. For instance, suppose you find yourself drawn to the swine building at the county fair (you may even want to show your own hogs someday). Wouldn't you appreciate a prize-winning purebred Landrace more if you knew a little about its heritage? Also, in some cases, breed registration is a required formality of exhibiting your animals.

Another reason for familiarizing yourself with the most common swine breeds is in case you have a choice about whether to raise this breed or that. Some hogs, Durocs and Duroc crosses for example, grow faster on less feed. Others, such as the Landrace and the Yorkshire, are noted for being good, high-producing mothers, which might affect your choice as a breeder, but not as a pork raiser.

Finally, a general knowledge of breeds will certainly help you if you decide to expand your pig-raising operations someday to include farrowing a sow or keeping a boar.

The following breeds are the most common in the United States and abroad. A short review of each will provide background which might be helpful in your weaner pig selection. More detailed information can be obtained from the breed registration associations listed in Appendix C.

Berkshire

One of the oldest breeds, the Berkshire, originated and was developed in the Shire of Berks, England. Animals of this breed have been exported from England world-wide.

Mature Berkshires are medium-size, generally smooth, solid hogs. Their suitable length and depth produce a good quality, meaty carcass.

Berkshires are characteristically black with white feet and a spot of white on the face. The original Berkshires were reddish or sandy and sometimes spotted. The head is distinctive with a slightly "dished" face that looks like a pug dog. Their ears are erect and the snout is medium in length.

Berkshires are hardy and rugged and can withstand the pressures of confinement living.

Chester White

An American breed, the Chester White originated in Chester County, Pennsylvania. Large, coarse hogs were crossed with smaller hogs to produce the modern medium-size version.

Chesters are the most durable of the white breeds, favored by meat packers because of their excellent "cutability" (the amount of lean, salable meat). They have lop (forward flopping) ears.

An offshoot of the Chester White is the OIC, Ohio Improved Chester.

Berkshire Gilt (Photo courtesy USDA)

Duroc Barrow (Photo courtesy USDA)

Yorkshire Gilt (Photo courtesy American Yorkshire Club)

Duroc

The pure red Duroc breed originated in the Northeast. It was originally a cross between 2 strains of red hogs, one developed in New Jersey (Jersey Reds) and the other in New York. The New York breed was supposedly developed by a man who owned a noted stallion named Duroc and, hence, the name was given to his special hogs. The resulting cross of the 2 breeds was known as Duroc-Jerseys, but the "Jersey" part was dropped to avoid confusion with the breed of cattle by the same name.

The Duroc breed is always red although the shade may vary from light to dark. They have floppy lop ears.

This breed is highly respected for aggressive, durable boars and productive, prolific females. It has been nicknamed the "growth breed" because the rugged, heavy boned, durable pigs grow to market weight faster than almost any other breed. Durocs adapt well to any environment.

Hampshire

The Hampshire breed may well be one of the oldest early American breeds of hogs existing today. Originating in Hampshire County, England, this is one of America's most popular breeds and the pork industry leader in leanness.

Early members of this breed were known as "Thin-Rind" because of their lack of backfat and thin skin. Originally, only Hampshire hogs were used for the famous Smithfield ham.

Hampshires are distinctively marked by a white belt that encircles a black body at the front legs. Smooth in appearance with medium-weight bones and erect ears, Hampshires are alert and active and show good foraging ability. Today, the breed is genetically faster-growing, leaner, and totally more efficient than in the past.

Yorkshire

Originating in or around Yorkshire County, England, some 200 years ago, the Yorkshire breed was first called the Large Whites. Although white is still the predominant color, Yorkshires occasionally have black spots in the skin.

The longest of all breeds, Yorkshires have small erect ears and short snouts. Sows of this breed farrow and raise large litters and hence their nickname the "Mother Breed." There are more Yorkshires in the United States than any other registered breed.

Landrace

One of the newer breeds of swine, the American Landrace are descendents of a Danish breed imported in the early 1930s. They are white with large, floppy lop ears that seem to cover their eyes. Landrace hogs have the largest ears of all the breeds. They have good body length for lots of bacon and chops.

Landrace hogs are noted for having the highest number of pigs per litter, high birth weights, and good milking abilities. Sows are docile and easily managed.

Poland China and Spot or Spotted

Surprisingly, Poland China hogs originated in neither Poland nor China, but rather in Butler and Warren Counties, Ohio. This breed is the result of several crossings, but the word "Poland" can be traced to a farmer who was of Polish descent and "China" from the original name, "Big China," which may or may not have any relationship to the country.

Poland China hogs are usually black but many are spotted with white. In fact, the *Spot* breed was first called the Spotted Poland China because it is exactly like the Poland China in body type but has more numerous white spots.

Lean, sturdy, adaptable, and showing efficient weight gains, the Poland China and Spot breeds have lop ears.

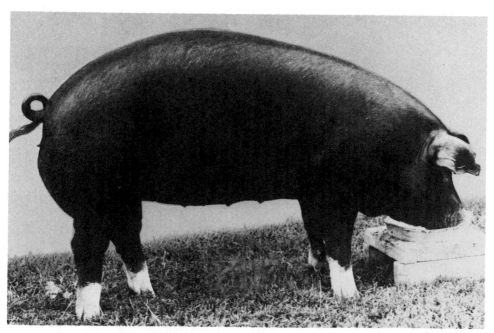

Poland China Gilt (Photo courtesy USDA)

Other Breeds

The Hereford hog has white markings on a red body similar to Hereford cattle. Several breeds already discussed, including the Duroc, Chester White, and Poland China, were used in developing the Hereford breed.

The Tamworth is one of the oldest of all hog breeds with purebreds dating back 150 years or more. The name was derived from the town of Tamworth in Staffordshire, England. Tamworth hogs are varying shades of red with erect ears and long snouts.

As a result of intensive breeding research, a number of inbred lines have been developed from crosses of 2 or more breeds. These inbreds have their own registration society but are not yet recognized as purebreds.

CROSSBREEDS

As mentioned earlier, only 10 percent of all hogs are purebred. These are called "seedstock." The remaining 90 percent are the product of a crossbreeding between a female of one breed and male of another or, more likely, between a crossbred sow and a purebred boar.

The reason for crossbreeding is a phenomena called *heterosis*, or hybrid vigor. Crossbred pigs reach market weight sooner than purebreds on the same amount of feed. Further, a crossbred sow mated with a purebred boar will have larger litters with a lower death rate and higher weaning weights. Why are crossbreeds more efficient and durable? Nobody really can say, at least not in simple terms. Of course, selection and genetics play an important role. And crossbreeding combines the desirable characteristics of different breeds while, hopefully, lessening the undesirable traits. Further, hybrid vigor is not passed down to descendents. In other words, if 2 crossbred hogs showing vigor were mated, their descendents would likely not show heterosis.

Whatever the mechanisms involved, if you want a fast-growing, feed-efficient hog for home pork production, look for youngsters that are the result of crossbreeding between parents of completely different ancestry.

For further information about breeds, crossbreeds, and heterosis, contact your county extension agent, your state or local swine growers association, or the swine breed associations listed in Appendix C.

Because we are interested in animal breeds in general, we like to know what we're getting when we buy our weaner pigs. Although we raise only crossbreeds, we like to compare growth rates and feed efficiency from year to year. Most good hog farmers will keep accurate records of their hog matings and will be more than happy to tell you about your weaner pigs' ancestry.

The Pacific Northwest is not abundant in breed choices since it is not generally considered a pork-production area. Our exposure to the different breeds listed here has been limited to Yorkshires, Hampshires, and Durocs. We've found that our favorite is the Yorkshire/Duroc cross. They have sweet dispositions, good feed efficiency, and they grow quickly to market weight. They adapt easily to any environment we've offered them and we've never had an animal of this crossbreeding get ill. Although all our hogs have produced excellent-tasting meat, we seem to get more lean (especially bacon) and less fat with the Yorkshire/Duroc cross. Further, they come in a variety of colors from pure red to red and black spotted to a calico mix of red, black, and white. Sure, color may not affect the quality of pork you get, but it increases your satisfaction if you enjoy looking at your animals.

Now the choice is yours. Whether you base your weaner pig selection on performance statistics, neighborly advice, body coloring, or ear shape is entirely up to you. With a little understanding of breeds and breed characteristics under your belt, however, you will be even better prepared to make an intelligent decision.

Chapter 4

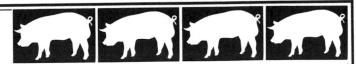

A PLACE
CALLED HOME:
HOUSING AND
PIGPEN BASICS

The first thing you should consider when thinking about raising your own pork is where you will house the hogs. Too many first-time raisers figure makeshift pens and inadequate shelters and fencing will suffice. Not true. Good sanitation and management are needed even with 2 or 3 animals. Although pigs are remarkably flexible and can tolerate a wide variety of housing conditions from pasture to complete confinement, don't expect quality meat from an animal raised in filth.

Further, bear in mind that your porker will change considerably during the finishing period. As a 40-pound weaner, he will be able to squeeze through small openings; as a 200-pound hog, he will tear down walls and root under fences. Build sturdy and not too small.

Also, consider location: Where is the water and feed? How close is the pen to human housing (is it downwind?)? To prevent unwanted odors, try to locate the pen at least 500 feet away from human dwellings. How is the drainage? Is there truck access, especially at butcher time? Is manure removal convenient to the compost pile? Lots of considerations, you say? Yes, indeed—and even more. Hence, take some time to consider proper housing before you bring Porky home.

The type of housing and pen you select as well as the space required will depend to a large extent on your management techniques, how many hogs you raise, and the environmental conditions. In all cases, as a bare minimum, pigs need protection from drafts, snow, and rain; shade in hot weather; and a dry sleeping area.

This simple framed pig hutch provides shade for pigs on pasture. Note that the bottom consists of skids to make moving easy.

SWINE HOUSING MANAGEMENT STYLES

Housing for your pigs can be as simple as a piece of plywood propped against a fence or as highly technical and complex as a computer-controlled totally enclosed confinement building. The management system you choose is dependent on your finances, time, and how many hogs you plan to raise. Your system will determine how your pigs will live, as well as your fencing, building materials, and daily labor requirements.

Selecting a housing management system will depend on several factors: First, consider your land and any outbuildings you have available. If you have a building, but little pasture or other livestock areas, space becomes an important element in your plans. You might want to consider the confined or modified confinement systems. On the other hand, if you have adequately fenced pasture or a few acres of underbrush that need to be cleaned up, then you should think about using a pasture or modified pasture (land-clearing) system.

The next factor to weigh when planning hog housing is how much money you have available to spend. If you want or need to house your hogs completely inside a building, but you don't have an acceptable hog house available, building one will be very expensive. On the other hand, a land-clearing pigpen with temporary fencing and a portable shed built of recycled materials can be almost free.

Next, take a look at the amount of time you want to spend on the daily housing needs of your animals. Although totally enclosed confinement buildings are usually designed to save the labor of the raiser, daily checks of heating/cooling systems, ventilation, and herd health (crowded confined hogs get sick more often than those with more space) are absolutely essential. Further, confined animals in a limited amount of space must have manure and other waste removed frequently unless expensive slotted floors are used. On the other hand, pastured animals and land-clearing hogs may not require manure removal or environmental controls, but they will need to have their fencing checked daily for areas that allow escape.

No matter which housing system you select, expect to spend some time each day with routine management procedures, such as replacing soiled bedding, repairing worn building materials, and removing wastes. Sorry, but there isn't a system that does it all for you.

Finally, think about housing in terms of the size of your hog-raising operation. Most small-scale (2 or 3 pigs a year) raisers don't invest in expensive hog set-ups, but rather use portable sheds with temporarily fenced lots or pasture areas. Also, because these hogs usually are not raised during the cold of the winter, sheds are designed to provide shade rather than warmth.

HOUSING AND MANAGEMENT OVERVIEW

In an attempt to help you with your housing and management decisions, we will describe the 3 most popular hog housing systems used today: totally confined, modified confinement, pasture, and land-clearing. Following this brief overview, we will discuss each system in detail.

The fully automated, highly mechanized, enclosed *total confinement system* is used mainly by large commercial operations that raise pigs year-round and often breed animals as well as produce pork.

The advantages of such a system are less daily labor is required; many pigs can be raised without much land; slotted floors make manure removal easy; temperature control minimizes or eliminates the need for bedding; and, complete control of the environment is in the hands of the farmer, rather than "Mother Nature's."

The disadvantages are high initial construction expense; odor control is often difficult; lack of sunlight and natural, unprocessed foods requires vitamin supplements in feed; disease can spread rapidly and can be caused by the stress of overcrowding; pigs massed together in a small amount of space can get very noisy, destructive, and vicious to each other, their pens, and their raiser; and, finally, the pigs are not allowed to express their natural rooting and grazing tendencies which may contribute to stress.

We do not recommend this system for anyone who plans to raise only a couple of hogs each year.

Modified confinement is popular with both large-scale and small-scale hog raisers. It consists of a permanent housing building and a fenced outside pen or run area. The floors of both the house and pen are commonly made of concrete and usually are slanted toward a drainage ditch for waste run-off. The modified confinement method can be altered to accommodate 2 pigs (a little brick shed with a small pen) or 200 (several housing units together, each with its own outside run). Further, this system can be used at all times of the year with efficient inside heating, cooling, and ventilation.

Although somewhat expensive to build initially, a well-constructed permanent pen can be expected to last through 5 to 10 years worth of hogs. This is a good housing management technique for the 2-hog pork raiser who doesn't want to move the animals, section by section, around a pasture or clearing lots, or for one who has only limited land available for hogs.

The *pasture system* allows hogs to freely graze within a fenced field. Housing, designed mainly to provide shade, is very simple and portable because the animals must be moved periodically from field to field to prevent pasture crop damage.

Although some large-scale commercial producers use the pasture system during all or parts of the year, it is best suited for the small-scale hog raiser with plenty of good pasture land, but not much money for housing construction.

There are several advantages to the pasture system. Grazing on good pasture will decrease feed requirements by 10 to 20 percent; vitamins from the vegetation and minerals from the soil eliminate the need for supplements; overcrowding, stress, and disease are rarely a problem; initial building and equipment expenses are less than with confined methods. A lower level of management skill and expertise is required and manure is automatically distributed. The system is well-suited to a small-scale operation and, it makes efficient use of available pasture land.

The disadvantages to pasture method are that more labor is required if feed and water are brought to the animals daily, and moving the shelter and the hogs requires occasional labor. If the pasture is damaged by rooting or wallow-building, animals will need to be ringed. Also it is often harder to restrain animals for medical examinations or medication.

This overview of the 3 housing management systems should give you some idea of which is right for your hog raising operation. The following in-depth descriptions of the methods most appropriate for the small-scale raiser offer more details to help you with your housing plans.

MODIFIED CONFINEMENT SYSTEMS

Many hog farmers prefer to utilize modified indoor systems, using permanently located inside pens with outdoor runs. These houses conserve space while still allowing the animal access to the outdoors.

Modified confinement pens usually don't make extensive use of environmental controls, but some heating and ventilation is generally required if the building is large. Small buildings can make efficient use of natural vents and bedding materials, such as straw and hay, for animal warmth.

Solid, sloping concrete floors (generally used inside and out for easy waste removal) and expensive automatic feeding and watering systems are preferred by large-scale producers to reduce the amount of daily labor required. Small-scale producers can use flat floors of dirt, wood, or concrete (or a combination of floor types) and feed and water can be brought to the animals daily.

Most experts recommend at least 6 square feet inside and the same amount of space outside for each animal. Although this arrangement is often possible for small-scale producers, large-scale operations often crowd animals together in far less space. As with the confinement system, pork animals are generally massed in group pens; only breeding and birthing hogs are allowed individual areas. This overcrowding leads to the same problems found in confinement systems: disease, stress, and destructiveness.

Because solid floors are used with a limited pen space, manure must be removed often (once a day to once a week, depending on pen size and number of animals housed together). Cleaning is usually accomplished by washing sloping concrete floors with a hose and broom. A sloping gutter at the bottom of the slanting pen carries manure to a holding lagoon. With flat floors and dirt pens, manure is removed with a shovel before the area is hosed or raked clean.

A solidly constructed, simple hog house can be used for 1 or 2 pigs. Durable and easy to clean, the illustrated unit features an automatic watering system, covered feeding area, concrete floors that slant to a holding pit at the front of the pen, draft-free sleeping quarters with a door that can be opened from outside the pen for ventilation, and hog-tight fencing anchored in the concrete flooring.

Modified confinement systems require more labor to clean, more bedding to keep the hogs warm in cold weather, and there is a greater risk of fly-related problems than with total confinement methods. However, the buildings are not as expensive to construct or maintain, ventilation problems are minimized, and the hogs have access to fresh air and sunshine.

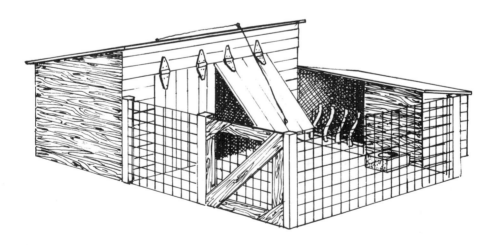

Even more elaborate pig shelters, complete with door, movable sides, and a floor, can be built on skids.

Fencing for outside runs is a problem that confinement raisers don't need to worry about; and hog-tight enclosures are neither easy nor cheap. Most large-scale producers using concrete outdoor runs anchor woven wire fencing into the concrete, but more about proper hog fencing at the end of this chapter.

UNCONFINED METHOD: HOGS ON PASTURE

There's much to be said for raising your pigs the way grandpa did, on the land. Swine require less pasture per head than other livestock. The protein and vitamins in the green forage and minerals in the soil provide high-quality nutrients and decrease feed consumption by 10 to 20 percent. Manure is automatically distributed over the land and generally does not have to be removed, which decreases labor requirements. Less tail/ear biting, foot/leg problems, and stress-related diseases occur on pasture. And with sanitation improved, diseases are easier to control.

Hogs make good gains on pasture, although not as fast as those housed in confinement or modified confinement buildings. This is probably because pastured pigs get more exercise and part of their feed goes to produce energy instead of meat or fat.

Although hogs will prosper on nearly any type of pasture, they do best if you plant the area with special crops before they arrive. The best legumes for hog pasture are ladino clover and alfalfa. Also, a special hog pasture mixture that contains 11 different seed varieties is available.

The pasture crop should be established in the fall on well-drained land, following a spring crop of wheat, oats, barley, peas, or early potatoes. Seed 3 pounds of clover or 15 pounds of alfalfa per acre and fertilize according to soil requirements. The clover should be 6 to 8 inches tall and the alfalfa a foot high before the pigs are allowed to graze.

Although up to 35 finishing hogs can graze an acre of good legume pasture, try to limit the herd to 10 or fewer per acre (about 20 square feet per animal) to prevent overgrazing. One pasture should then last from early spring (February or March in the Pacific Northwest) to late June.

Do not graze hogs on the same pasture every year. Alternate the hogs with hay or other livestock. Rotating pastures aids in parasite control and also gives the land a chance to heal from rooting damage. Although many pigs will be satisfied to simply graze the surface of the pasture, some insist on digging it up to get at tender roots and earthworms. Further, most pigs will dig into the shallow-rooted clover more than the alfalfa. Very destructive hogs, especially mature boars and sows, may need to have their noses ringed to prevent excess pasture damage.

Ringing a hog's nose is not a hard procedure and certainly no more painful that piercing human ears. One or two small rings are placed above each nostril, on the edge of the rooter (the hard ring of cartilage) or through the tissue between the nostrils. Rings and ringing tools are available from most farm supply stores.

For growing and finishing pigs, 1 ring in the center of the nose is sufficient. Sows may need 2 or 3 rings. Breeding boars must not be rung because the rings may interfere with the mating process and actually injure the female (as part of courtship, males root at the females' external genital organs).

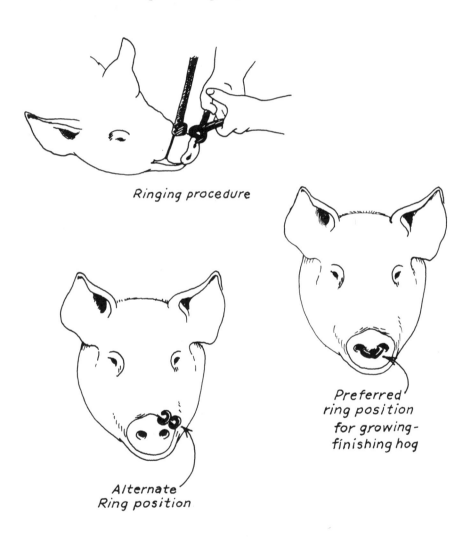

Ringing procedure

Preferred ring position for growing-finishing hog

Alternate Ring position

Ringing a pig.

Pastured swine need adequate shelter and bedding, shade, and sufficient fresh water, especially during extremely warm weather. Most hogs will dig themselves a *wallow* during hot spells. Wallows are nothing more than deep mudholes which can virtually destroy a pasture. If ponds or streams are available in the pasture, the hogs might try cooling off in them as well. Not only does this cause bank erosion but it may contribute to the spread of intestinal parasites. Satisfactory cooling substitutes are concrete wallows, sprinklers, and plenty of drinking water and shade. Some hogs, however, will find a way to tip their water trough and dig a cool mudhole, despite all efforts to stop them. Ringing the nose may be the only way to stop this digging.

Extremely simple housing will suffice for pastured pigs in the mild spring through fall season. Quite simply, all they really need is a roof over their heads (mainly for shade), protection from drafts (3-sided buildings are sufficient), and dry bedding. Allow a 5-foot × 5-foot sleeping area for each hog if possible. They'll need that much room by the time they reach butcher size and overcrowding causes stress-related problems. Six inches of bedding (straw, hay, sawdust, or dry leaves) is important, especially if the building is floorless. Pigs enjoy making nests in their bedding for warmth. Old bedding can be used to soak up urine or excess water in the manure area.

An A-frame structure is easy to construct, inexpensive, and makes efficient use of materials. We recommend a shelter similar to this for a 2-pig pasture operation. Further, a unit such as this is portable and can be rotated with the hogs from pasture to pasture. Larger houses, with or without floors, can be built on skids and moved by tractor, truck, or horse. For more detailed construction information for portable hog shelters, see Appendix A.

Pastures for hogs have the disadvantage of requiring much hog-tight fencing. Because the animals have more room to move about and tend to entertain themselves better in a pasture, chances are their escape efforts will be fewer than those of pigs in small pens. However, boredom will set in eventually and with boredom comes escape attempts.

If any area of the pasture becomes muddy, overgrazed, or dug up, move the swine to a new area. This is easily accomplished if the pasture areas are close to each other. First move the hogs' shelter and feed and watering equipment. Then, serve dinner in the new location when you are sure the animals are hungry. With 2 or 3 pigs, this task can be accomplished by 1 or 2 persons. With more hogs, you may need some additional helpers on moving day. (See chapter 7 for more suggestions regarding herding hogs.)

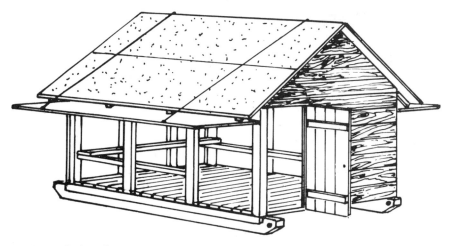

A simple hog house

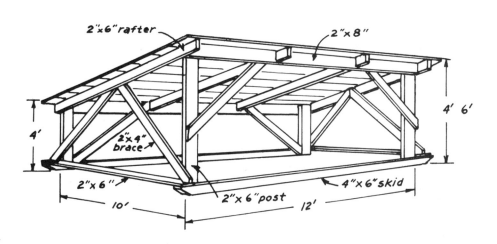

2"x 6" rafter

2" x 8"

4' 6'

4'

2"x 4" brace

2" x 6"

4" x 6" skid

2" x 6" post

10'

12'

A simple hog shelter

MODIFIED PASTURE METHOD: LAND-CLEARING OPERATIONS

Most hog-raisers overlook a benefit when they confine their pigs to indoor houses, concrete pens, or legume pasture. Hogs like to dig. Their snouts are designed for digging. Given the opportunity, nothing keeps a pig happier than rooting.

Our forefathers realized that their hogs could help clear the forest lands. At first, it was by accident. Pig raisers ran the swine through the forest to eat nuts and seeds in the fall of the year, a tradition called *masting*. Then, when the food on top of the forest floor ran out, the farmers noticed that the hogs were digging up the soil and destroying even the tough, prickly briars and other fast-spreading bushes in a matter of weeks.

Hog-tillers will bring even giant rocks to the surface. They destroy and eat root systems that couldn't be broken up without a bulldozer. They can even unearth large trees and stumps if you hide corn or other goodies in deep holes near the roots. Further, turned into a potato or root crop field after the human harvest, pigs will feed themselves with what remains, clearing the land in the process. What is left behind is well-turned, manured, vegetation-clear land that you can use as lawn, garden, pasture, or whatever you like.

Hog-tilling operations are especially valuable in rough, rocky, brushy land where human clearing is extremely labor-intensive or requires expensive machinery.

To be most effective, pigs must be confined to their work area (generally no larger than 20 feet by 20 feet for 2 or 3 pigs) for at least 2 to 3 weeks to complete their clearing operation. Confining hogs in land-clearing lots is not always an easy task, however, especially if the land is hilly or covered with thick undergrowth.

Single-strand electric or barbed wire fences, although not generally recommended, might work until the animals tire of their pen and decide the grass looks greener on the other side of the hot wire. We've found that relatively small, portable yards (created with movable, temporary fencing) work best, even when a little human labor must be expended to situate the fence.

Hog panels, 16-foot sections of welded steel rods which attach to steel fence posts, are one solution. Another is to create or scavenge wood panels, pallet boards, or other easily moved fence sections which can be tied or nailed to steel or wooden fence posts. A third option is to alternate electric and barbed wire strands, at least one of each (2 or more is better), strung between metal posts no further than 10 feet apart, but more on fencing at the end of this chapter.

The main idea with a land-clearing hog pen is to temporarily confine the hogs in a given area until they have completely cleared it of vegetation. Then, move them to a second pen constructed next to the first, and then to a third pen using the fencing from the first one. By always using the 2-pen system as shown below, you never find yourself with cleared land and nowhere to move the hogs without freeing them.

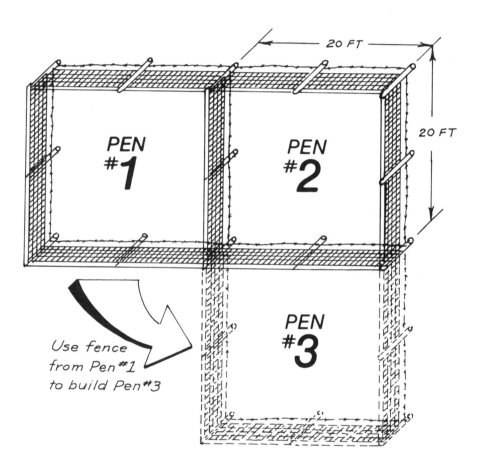

The 2–pen clearing method.

Not only should the pen's fencing be portable and reusable, but so should the very simple housing. Again, the A-frame is ideal but you don't even need to get that complex. Considering that the animals are going to be moved every month or so, a roof (for shade and protection from rain) and several inches of dry bedding are all they need in mild weather.

A friend of ours has a novel way to make use of his hogs' land-clearing potential, while still using an available confinement housing building. He tethers his pigs during the day, much like a dog, using light chain (pigs will chew rope) and a harness (using belly, behind the front legs, and/or neck straps). A swivel at one end of the chain prevents twisting. He uses a simple lean-to structure for shade or he ties them near a protective tree. He also makes clean water available in a large bucket. Using the chain as a leash and a bucket of food as incentive, he slowly guides them back and forth from the building each day. The hardest part, he says, is moving them back to the building in the evening (apparently, they like rooting better than confinement).

A few words of warning about hog-tiller operations, especially when running hogs through heavy growth areas. Some common plants can be quite poisonous to hogs. These include the cocklebur, nightshade family members, water hemlock, buttercup, tarweed, St. John's wart, and rhubarb leaves. Although the toxicity of these plants is somewhat dependent on the amount ingested, they should be avoided when situating the pen. If you're not sure what is growing out there, give a call to your local extension agent or toxic weed specialist.

If the area the swine are clearing becomes muddy, move them to a new pen area. Filthy, muddy, damp conditions usually mean disease won't be far behind.

FENCING

Whether you use the modified confinement system with an outdoor run, the pasture system, or land-clearing lots, you have to consider how you will keep your hogs in their pens. Hence, fencing is a crucial, and sometimes difficult and expensive, housing consideration.

Small, feeder pigs are easier to fence than strong, mature hogs, but all swine root and rub and bite at everything. Fences must be sturdy.

Most enclosures should be at least 3 feet high. However, some pigs, especially those with limited outdoor run areas, become good jumpers or climbers. We once had a hog named "Dufus" who managed to climb every fence we put between him and the outside world. If someone tells you that hogs don't jump fences, don't you believe it! Most hogs don't—but some will. To be on the safe side, all hog fences should be 3 to 4 feet high with a strand of electric or barbed wire near the top to discourage climbing.

Board fences will work if the lumber is solid and strong and placed on the **inside** of the posts. Pigs will push a fence apart if the boards are nailed to the outside. Also, consider barbed or electric wire near ground level. We've found pigs can and will root under board fences faster then wire ones.

Hog-tight woven wire fencing is best, but expensive. It usually comes in a 32-inch height, which is a little low for the rare jumping or climbing pigs you may encounter. Barbed or electric wire can be strung along the top to discourage this habit. Barbed or electric wire also should be placed about 2 to 3 inches from the ground to discourage rooting under the fenceline, unless the fence is anchored solidly in concrete. Or logs can be used around the bottom of the fence, but be sure that they are attached securely to the fence. You'd be surprised how strong pigs are; rolling logs is not beyond their capability.

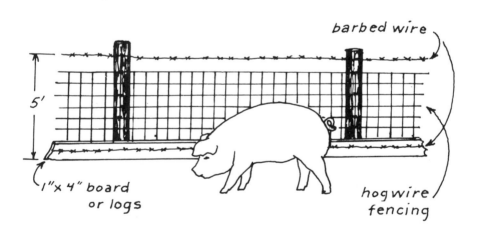

Fencing must be sturdy. A combination of woven hog wire (nailed to the inside of the posts), barbed wire (strung 2 to 3 inches above the fencing and 2 to 3 inches above the ground), and boards or logs on the bottom of pen should keep the hogs confined.

Some hog farmers suggest using 1 or 2 strands of electric or barbed wire instead of a regular fence. Despite the inexpensiveness and ease of installation, we don't recommend this. We've seen too many escaped pigs who were penned in this manner. The little ones squeeze under; the big guys go right through.

Nonetheless, we've been assured that if you train baby pigs to hot wire, they will respect it when they grow up. Raisers we've spoken to who use only electric wire say that they train piglets to respect their electric enclosures by touching each piglet's nose to the wire. The sudden shock teaches the piglet that wire hurts and supposedly he will never get close to it again.

We still have our doubts about using electric or barbed wire alone. Perhaps it depends on how much the hog wants to leave his area (pigs are less likely to escape from larger pens), but the brief shock of an electric fence or the momentary prick of barbed wire won't deter a 200-pound porker who has visions of rooting up your garden. Unless you enjoy trying to coax an escaped hog back into his pen, don't use makeshift fencing in the first place – even if it is cheap and easy to put up.

Steel or wooden fenceposts for swine fencing should be no more than 10 feet apart, preferably 5 to 7 feet apart. Although limiting the number of posts decreases the expense of hog fences, it also decreases the sturdiness. Don't skimp!

We've used many different fence types and methods, but we have concluded that we like a "semi-solid" fence best with our land-clearing pens. Our hogs seem to respect an enclosure that they can actually see and walk up to and touch. With this method, we use scrap boards or field fence (about 3½ feet high) as the main enclosure. It is attached securely to the inside of split cedar posts. Around the top and bottom, on the inside, we string 1 strand of barbed or electric wire to discourage jumping over or rooting under. A gate (recycled yard type or even a pallet board with hinges, attached securely to posts) allows us easy access for feeding and cleaning. Most of our hogs have been satisfied to stay put with this method.

Of course, we've had an occasional climber or digger who was not deterred by the strands of barbed and electric wire and managed to escape. For this reason, we recommend that you don't take your fences for granted. One of your daily chores should be a careful fence check: If there are any areas where the hogs are digging under, fill the holes with packed-down dirt or rocks or a combination of dirt and rocks. If one particular hog climbs, consider adding electric wire at the top or making your fence higher. If your fenceposts are falling apart, replace them. A few minutes spent each day on fence repairs could save you many hours of chasing escaped pigs or of needing to replace the fence entirely.

If you want or need more information about constructing a hog shelter or fencing, we've included some building ideas and other information in Appendix A. Your local extension agent, neighboring hog farmers, and construction firms specializing in farm buildings are also good sources of information.

Ultimately, your hog housing choice will depend on your goals, available money and labor, and the number of pigs you need to house. But regardless of the housing system used, the level of success is a function of your skill with animal management and your attention to the details of cleanliness, eliminating stress, and protecting the health of your hogs.

Chapter 5

BRINGING
HOME THE BACON:
BUYING PIGLETS

So you think you're ready for the big step: buying weaner pigs. You've checked with local extension agents and you know that the law is on your side and you're ready now, right? Well, hold on a minute more. Before you go hog hunting, better make sure you have a place for the miniature porkers that is secure, clean, and will accommodate a 200-plus-pound market hog as well as a 30-pound youngster. Nothing is more frustrating than trying to catch a frightened, squealing piglet—an almost impossible task!

Just to prove the point a little further, our neighbors were the perfect example of what not to do. They thought that they were all set for the arrival of 2 little oinkers into their life. No legal restrictions, and they had a nice little pen surrounded by electric wire. The only problem was that the wire was too far off the ground. It was perfect for a larger hog, but the tiny piggies slipped right under with nary a squeal.

Hours later, our neighbors noticed the 2 weaners curled up in a clump of long grass some distance from their pen. In a panic and thinking only of the money invested in the porkers, man, wife, 2 children, and several neighbors began a wild chase. One piglet was recaptured — barely. The other escaped into the forest, never to be heard from again, despite an extensive search. It probably was an unexpected pork dinner for a hungry coyote. Our neighbors were out the price of a weaner pig, complaining that they didn't know swine were so small at that age. They learned their lesson and replaced the electric wire with weaner-proof fence.

Moral of the story: Be prepared! Makeshift, inappropriate housing won't work. Remember that your new piggies are very frightened anyway when they first arrive at your place. They don't know you yet and, further, they don't trust you at all! If they escape under, over, or through the pen, chances are you won't catch them. So don't fake it! If you don't already have an appropriate pigpen area, please return to chapter 4 to learn the do's and don't's of making one. If you do have a used pigpen — perhaps you have raised your own pork before or someone before you left one behind — clean it thoroughly and then clean it some more. Baby pigs, stressed from moving to a new home, are especially vulnerable to getting sick.

Cleaning the pigpen area doesn't require anything fancy. Soap and water will suffice. However, special disinfectants are usually available at feed stores or you can pick up a bottle of household disinfectant from the local grocer.

Use hot water to make a solution with your chosen cleaner. A stiff-bristled brush is a must to get into all the cracks and crevices, especially when cleaning wood or rough concrete. Find one with a long pole if you don't like cleaning on your hands and knees. You can rinse down the scrubbed area with a garden hose if you desire, but a hot-water rinse is most effective.

After all your cleaning is finished, let the pen air dry for a few days before putting animals in it. This will not only help eliminate any chemical odor that might remain, but it will dry up damp areas. Also, old-fashioned sunshine is nature's very best all-purpose disinfectant!

All right, now you're ready.

FINDING WEANER PIGS

Probably the best place to buy weaner pigs is from a good neighbor or local producer. But, get to know the breeders and their facilities before you lay down cash. Ask around to find out if the seller's reputation is good and whether he or she offers only sound, healthy piglets. Go to feed stores, other raisers, veterinarians, and custom slaughterhouses to get their suggestions. Then shop around. Check the livestock categories in the local newspaper want ads. Compare quality and prices. Don't ever assume a piglet from a dirty, unkempt pig lot will straighten out when you get it home. Chances are it won't.

If you plan to raise your pigs outside, buy from a producer who raises outside. The piglets might already be immune to soil-borne diseases in your area.

Your last resort is to buy at a livestock auction. Here, baby pigs are already stressed by the move and unfamiliar surroundings. Further, they are exposed to all kinds of germs and disease brought in by other animals. The temptation to save money at auctions is great. However, odds are good that your new purchase, no matter how low the price, will cost more in time and medicines to bring it back to health than a full-priced piglet from a reliable local breeder. Another factor against auctions is that you have no way to judge the piglet's parents or the farm where it was born. Quite frankly, when you buy at auctions, you get a "pig in a poke" ("poke" is an old term for bag or sack).

WHAT TO LOOK FOR WHEN SELECTING PIGLETS

Weaners, feeders, shoats, and feeder pigs are one and the same animal. They are weaned piglets, usually 6 to 8 weeks old, weighing at least 30 to 40 pounds. The "standard weight" is 40 pounds, but the feeder pig class varies widely from early-weaned to half-finished. In 1984, we expected to pay about $1 a pound for healthy weaner pigs in our area of the country.

Choose the healthiest, happiest, biggest, and best cared-for pigs you can find. They should be alert and active, running when you touch them and squealing when caught. Look for a smooth, shiny coat with a healthy pink skin color (not anemic white) and no protruding backbone or flat sides. If the tails have not been docked by the raiser, look for a tightly curled up tail, a sure sign of a happy pig.

Piglets should have no signs of disease such as diarrhea, swollen leg joints, coughs or sneezing, matted eyes, abscesses, hernia, droopy tail, limping, or shaking. You may feel sorry for the sick little guys and want to "mother" them, but do yourself a favor and don't take problems home.

Pick the biggest pigs in the litter, if you can. Generally, the larger a pig is at weaning, the faster it will grow to market weight. You might be tempted to take home a runt pig much smaller than its litter mates, especially if the raiser almost gives him to you free. Resist the temptation. Runts take a very long time to grow to market weight, if they make it. Further, they may never be strong or healthy because of their bad start.

We go piglet-shopping in the early spring. Although we may visit several local raisers, we've purchased from one nearby farmer for many years. He raises Yorkshires and Durocs that have won many awards and trophies at local and state fairs. We are always impressed with the cleanliness and efficiency of his operation, as well as the friendliness of his animals. He has a Duroc boar the size of a hippopotamus who is as gentle as a puppy and loves to have his ears scratched.

The producer we buy from keeps his weaner pigs that are for sale in a separate, heated building. This is where we go to make our selection, although we may spend some time visiting with his other animals and watching the newborn piglets first. We also spend some time talking about the breeding background of the weaners before we visit them.

Once in the weaner building, we look at all the piglets and rule out those who seem smaller, slower, or poorly shaped. When we have narrowed the field down to a dozen or less, the producer helps by catching the finalists one at a time for a closer inspection. We eliminate those who don't scramble away from his grasp or squeal loudly when caught.

Finally, the field is down to 4 or 5 prime little piglets. Now what? We only want to raise 2 porkers. This is where our subjective decisions come in. If one has a coat color more interesting than another, choice is based on color, which has nothing to do with meat. If that one has a cute little face and giant ears, he may get selected simply for that reason. If another has a kink in his tail or some other minor deformity, that may be enough reason to eliminate it from consideration.

When we have eventually chosen our 2 weaner pigs, the producer marks their backs with a grease pencil to indicate that they are ours. If the piglets are at least 8 weeks of age, we may take them home right then and there after paying the raiser. If, as usually happens with this producer, the piglets are only 5 or 6 weeks old, we give the raiser a "holding fee" (usually 10 to 25 percent of the selling price) and leave them where they are for at least another 2 or 3 weeks. When we return to take them home, we pay the producer the rest of the money.

Other Factors to Consider When Selecting Piglets

The best raisers routinely castrate males before they sell them as feeder pigs. A male pig that has not been castrated may have pork with an undesirable odor and flavor. Opinions vary as to whether castrated pigs grow faster than their uncastrated brothers. Some raisers state that the boar (uncastrated) grows faster; others say that the barrows (castrated) make better gains because they don't need to put their energy into developing sex organs. Most don't notice much difference—we haven't. In any case, choose barrows or gilts (young females) for pork production when possible. We've found that the aggressive, breeding-oriented temperament of a boar is a bigger reason to avoid raising one than the possibility that the meat may be tainted. Castrating your own males is another possibility, but it is not an easy procedure for beginners (see chapter 11).

Most raisers agree that barrows will eat and gain a little more than gilts, but we haven't noticed much difference. However, because females are often saved for future breeding, they may cost a little more.

Find out from the raiser if the piglets have been wormed and immunized against local disease. Many breeders do this, but some don't. If the pigs have not been immunized or wormed, but you are raising only 2 for your own pork, chances are good that they will not need these treatments. We've raised many porkers with no medications or immunizations and have had no problems at all. Breeding animals and large herds, on the other hand, do need to be routinely vaccinated and dewormed.

Ask to see the piglets' parents if they aren't readily available. Most good producers are more than happy to show off their stock and may even tell you more than you care to know about their operation. Although parent performance records aren't crucial if you are just producing pork, you may be interested anyway (we are) and most raisers are glad to brag a little.

When visually examining the weaner pigs' parents, look for long, lean hogs with large hams, sound legs and feet, and meaty sides. Remember that the babies are the product of the parents. Find out if the sow and boar are from completely different ancestry to give the piglets the benefit of hybrid vigor for faster growth and better feed efficiency. Most probably, the sow will be a crossbreed and the boar a purebred animal.

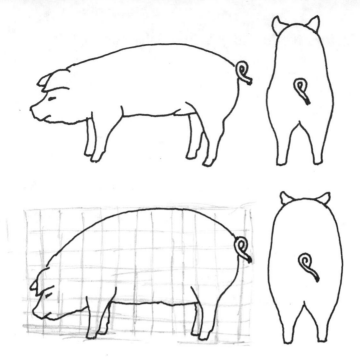

Good (top) versus poor form.

Grades of Feeder Pigs

The USDA grades feeder pigs from larger operations based on the expected slaughter quality of the resultant market hog. Although these grades are not so important to the small-scale pork producer, they may provide some insight concerning what traits to look for when selecting your weaners:

- **US #1: Very thick muscling, large frame, wide-set legs. The hams are wider than the loin. Trim with no excess fat.**
- **US #2: Moderate muscling and medium large frame. Hams slightly wider than loin. Jowl and flank slightly fatty.**
- **US #3: Smaller frame and thinner muscling. Uniform width through ham and loin. Relatively high degree of fatness.**
- **US #4: Thin muscling, small frame. Rather flat back. Uniform width through hams and loins. Fat at jowls, flank, lower hams.**
- **US UTILITY: Diseased or poor care. Wrinkled skin, rough appearance. Head appears larger than normal.**
- **US CULL: Very deficient. Expect long and costly feeding period. May not make it to market weight.**

HOW MANY PIGS TO RAISE

How many pigs to raise depends on you. How much room do you have? How much time and energy for daily chores? How much pork do you want to eat? Do you have a sure market for any excess?

Many first-time pork producers figure one pig at a time is the best way to go. However, there's a good argument for raising at least two.

Pigs are intelligent and social. They appreciate company and they like to curl up together to keep warm at night. One pig gets bored easily; two pigs will chase and play.

Two pigs are as easy to care for as one. When one eats, the other will, too. They argue over food and empty the trough just to keep the other from doing it. Two pigs together tend to grow faster and waste less feed than a single pig. Less wasted feed means fewer rat problems, which results in less disease.

Two pigs are easier to move than one. Where one goes, the other wants to go, too, and will often try to get there faster.

The average family of 4 to 6 persons can often eat one pig's worth of pork in 6 months. Two pigs provide enough for a full year. Or if your family eats less than average, part can be sold to defray the raising costs.

Two pigs are as easy to care for as one.

All right, you say, if 2 are better than one, I'll go whole hog and get 3 or 4 or more. Hold on! Unless you have a guaranteed market for all that pork (say, you're raising a couple for a relative), don't get caught in the same trap we found ourselves in a few years ago. Our luck with 2 pigs at a time over several years had been so good that we decided to try twice that many 1 year. We did not have sure buyers for the excess pork. Then the bottom dropped out of the local pork market, and we were stuck with virtually worthless pork at butchering day. We ended up giving most of the excess to friends and relatives because we didn't have room to store it. Take our advice, especially if you are a first-timer: two is plenty!

If you plan to raise more than one, be sure that the piglets you choose weigh within 5 pounds of each other. Pigs with widely varying weights will not work. The bigger ones will bully the little guys who may not grow properly.

COSTS FOR WEANER PIGS

Feeder pig prices vary widely by locale and time of year. Generally feeder pigs sell for about twice as much per pound as do market hogs. We paid $40 apiece for prime 8-week-old weaners in 1984. At the time, weaner pigs were selling locally for $25 to $50. The cost of weaner pigs can be as much as 40 percent of the investment you make in pork production.

Pricing is complex and is indirectly affected by the daily and weekly movement of live hogs, current slaughter prices, feed costs (especially corn prices), "hog cycle," supply and demand of hogs and pork, and the weather of the region.

To get an idea how much you should pay, keep track of auction or cooperative marketing reports. Both are commonly found in your local newspaper. Check the livestock want ads, too. Ask at feed stores what the going rate is.

Remember that you will probably pay the most for the best-raised pigs. That's because the money you give to the hog farmer pays for keeping the sow and the boar, the food the piglet eats, and all medications and surgical procedures the piglet received. Of course, this is not always the case. Some less-than-honest farmers will charge top dollar for poor quality, figuring you're pretty green and won't know the difference anyway. Don't buy it! Also, some raisers will charge you more than the bulk buyer who purchases hundreds of thousands of weaner pigs at a time. A 2-pig or 3-pig order is an irritant and you may be charged a "surtax" for being small. If that's the case, and you can't find another more reasonable seller, you may have to grin and bear it.

Several formula pricing variations can serve as a guide to what is a reasonable price to pay for a weaned feeder pig. Just remember that the figures you obtain are only indications, not a firm price. Fluctuations on an almost daily basis are common.

[50 %] × [price per 100 pounds of butcher hog] + [$4–5] = estimated cost of weaner pig

or

[feeder pig weight] × [1.6] × [current market price, per pound, for butcher hog] = estimated cost of weaner pig

Call a local hog buyer or packer or check the newspapers for the current butcher hog market price for these calculations.

Feeder pigs are most commonly sold by the head (as individuals); however, some are marketed like butcher hogs, by the pound. In 1984 in our area, $1 a pound for weaners was a fair price and anything less was a bargain. Some went for more, but we figured that there had to be a good reason to pay it. Just remember the consumer's golden rule: Let the buyer beware! Shop around. Get the best deal you can get and don't always accept the first offer you receive.

HOW TO GET PORKY HOME

Moving animals is never easy—on you or on the animals. Weaner pigs are no exception. Although the little guys are almost small enough to ride home on your lap, most people prefer to transport them in the bed of a pick-up truck. Some raisers suggest that the pigs are best moved in clean burlap bags, tied shut. Others suggest secure wooden boxes or cages.

It's true that piglets travel better in the dark. Further, restraining them with bags or boxes lessens the chances of them hurting themselves in a truck bed. However you manage the trip from the hog farm to your pen, the goal is to get the piglets home and into their new surroundings as quickly and efficiently as possible. "Shipping fever," a set of flu-like symptoms rather than a real disease, is always a possibility when an animal is subjected to the stress and trauma of moving.

We usually transport our new babies in the bed of our pick-up truck. We use a wooden canopy to provide protection, security, and darkness. Although we've tried burlap feed bags and wooden or cardboard boxes, we've found that a thick layer of straw in the truck bed works best. Slow, careful driving eliminates bouncing around. By the time we get home, the piglets have created a nest of hay in a far corner and buried themselves in it.

Once parked securely in your own driveway, you are faced with another problem: how to get that squealing, wriggling little piglet from the truck bed into the pigpen, especially if your driveway is some distance away. Most raisers suggest that you carry small pigs upside-down by their hind legs. This works. You can also try moving them in a box or feed bag if you aren't too sure of yourself or you absolutely can't stomach the squealing. In fact, if you boxed or bagged the piglets before driving them home, they can be moved to their pen, container and all, before being released. We've moved piglets successfully by simply holding them in our arms like puppies—some enjoy the cuddling and others will squirm and squeal like crazy. Whatever you do, do it fast and securely. Remember, a runaway piglet is probably a never-to-be-seen-again piglet!

Offer your new babies food and water immediately. We recommend that you bring home some of the same feed that the hog farmer was using and gradually change the ration to what you will use. Sudden shifts of diet, especially in young pigs and those already stressed by travel, can cause an often-fatal diarrhea.

Alter the diet in steps; use the familiar feed for at least the first week. Then mix it half and half with the ration you prefer to use for another week or two. Finally, feed your chosen menu alone. (Chapter 6 will go into more details about feeding.)

But back to your newly arrived piglets. Once they are watered and fed, go away and leave them alone for awhile to let them get accustomed to their environment. Yes, you can peek occasionally, but no handling and no loud noises. The pigs will probably stay huddled up in a corner or in their bed area for several hours, but soon they will begin to explore every square inch. Within a few weeks, they will no longer run away when they see you coming. Give them a little more time and they'll nibble your pants leg and call for you at mealtime. In a few months, when they've reached butcher weight, you'll almost have to beat them off with a stick.

Chapter 6

LIFE WITH PORKY PIG: DAILY MANAGEMENT AND FEEDING

All livestock require daily care. Your hogs are no exception. Much as you might wish that your pigs would raise themselves, no management system has been devised to eliminate all the labor on the raiser's part.

How much care your pigs need and what sorts of chores you must do every day depend a great deal on the type of housing arrangement your hogs have. Therefore, we have broken daily management into sections to correspond with the main types of housing.

DAY-TO-DAY MANAGEMENT IN CONFINEMENT AND MODIFIED CONFINEMENT HOUSING

Confinement buildings are designed mainly to save the manual labor of the raiser. However, there is a trade-off: Although labor-intensive operations such as feeding, watering, and manure-removal are minimized, the chores that must be attended to on a daily basis are highly technical. Each day, the producer must check environmental controls (heating, cooling, ventilation), manure flushing systems, automatic feed and water equipment (which are prone to clogging), and numerous other mechanical operations that could break down. Many times, these functions are controlled by a computer. Hence, besides technical and mechanical knowledge, the raiser may even need some computer expertise.

Further, crowded confinement facilities tend to stress animals, leading to a number of stress-related illnesses. Also, contagious diseases are spread from pig to pig very rapidly. Therefore, besides mechanical and technical knowledge, the producer also must be a veterinarian of sorts (large operations usually have an animal doctor employed on-site). Each day, he or she must check the herd for signs of health problems—which are common and varied. Sick or dead hogs must be removed from the group facilities and kept in separate quarters or properly disposed of.

Although most confinement and partial confinement systems make use of slotted floors for automatic manure and waste removal from the pens, some still use solid concrete. In this case, especially if many animals are housed together in limited space, manure build-up can be rapid. To minimize disease and odor problems, floors must be thoroughly scrubbed and hosed down at least once a day.

We do not recommend these systems for small-scale part-time raisers with limited money, limited time for daily chores, or limited livestock experience. Although confinement and semi-confinement methods look tempting at first, the expense and technical knowledge required to maintain a healthy herd under these conditions are considerable.

PASTURE MANAGEMENT

Many large-scale and small-scale hog producers raise their animals on pasture. Although some daily chores are minimized (manure is automatically distributed over the land to fertilize the pasture crops), others tend to be more time-consuming and difficult when animals are given lots of room to roam.

Probably the biggest chore required with pastured hogs is fence maintenance. Each day, you must examine the entire fencing sys tem for breaks, holes, and areas that might allow escape. We recommend that repairs be made immediately, as hogs seem to sense where the fence is weakest, and they could totally destroy it in a matter of days unless it is fixed quickly.

Because housing for pastured hogs is usually very simple, especially for those raised only during the warmest months of the year, complex environmental controls are rarely used. Hence, daily housing chores are reduced to simply checking the structure for leaks or deterioration. Again, if you want the shelter to last, make repairs immediately.

Also, if bedding such as straw or hay is used, it should be checked. If it seems muddy or wet, remove it from the housing and replace it with dry material. This chore is generally required about once a week unless the shelter roof leaks or the weather has been particularly damp. In that case, expect to change the bedding every few days.

An ample, clean water supply must be available to pastured animals at all times. Water troughs must be emptied daily and thoroughly scrubbed before refilling.

Even though pastured hogs are grazing and getting substantial nutrition from the grasses and soil, a grain-based feed must be available, too. Most raisers use a self-feeder that is large enough to hold about a week's worth of dry food. Daily checks should be made of the feeder unit to make sure it is not empty or clogged.

If you prefer to hand-feed your animals, you will have to bring their food to troughs (usually situated near the shelter) twice a day. Before the troughs are filled with new food, they must be rinsed clean of anything remaining from the previous feeding.

Finally, plan to watch your pastured hogs for a few minutes each day. Actually, this is an enjoyable chore because pigs are an interesting group of animals to watch — especially in a pasture where they have lots of room to romp and play. But while you are chuckling at their antics, be sure you check each pig for signs of illness. How are they eating? Has one or more "gone off feed" (refuses to eat)? Is one animal staying in the shelter all day? Do you notice any foot or leg injuries, limping, other signs of pain? If a hog seems to be sick, it should be isolated from the rest of the herd in a small pen. Then follow the recommendations in chapter 7 regarding when to call in expert medical help.

LAND-CLEARING LOT MANAGEMENT

This is the housing and management system that we use most often. With 4 acres of undeveloped underbrush needing to be cleared, we can take advantage of our hogs' natural rooting and digging instincts and save $40 an hour in bulldozing charges. Although daily chores are minimized to some extent with this system (housing is simple; manure is automatically taken care of; and feed is supplemented by soil and plant nutrients), day-to-day management skills are still required.

First and foremost each day is a fence checking and repair session. As with pastured pigs, maintaining a solid, undamaged barrier between the hogs and the outside world is always a prime chore. Electric fencing, if used, should be tested each day to make sure it is still operative (simple things like rain, vegetation, and even a wind storm can short the system and knock out the juice to your fence). If wood, field fencing, or portable fence panels are used, inspect every square inch for damage. Pay particular attention to the fence at ground level. Rooting hogs can dig a hole under the fenceline in a matter of hours. Refill all holes, preferably with a rock and dirt mix, and pack the soil down firmly with your boot. This will slow the animals up, but sometimes not very much. Barriers along the fence bottom (logs, wood planks, and electric or barbed wire) are recommended.

Next, check the shelter and bedding. Because land-clearing housing is so simple and portable, it can often be pushed apart—especially by large hogs—if you don't pay attention to daily repairs as they are needed. Check for roof leaks, loose nails, wobbly walls, and general sturdiness—and don't put off needed repairs.

Make sure that the bedding, usually straw or hay, is dry. If it is damp or if the animals have pushed it out of the shelter, replace it with plenty of dry material.

Wash and refill water troughs daily—more often if the animals seem to muddy their drinking water quickly. All hogs, no matter what housing arrangement you choose, must have access to clean drinking water at all times. This is particularly difficult in land-clearing lots, as the hog-tillers tend to toss rooted materials into the water troughs. Further, because the pens are relocated as the ground is cleared (about every 4 to 6 weeks), automatic watering systems won't work.

Clearing-lot hogs can be fed with self-feeders that hold several days' worth of dry food. Check them daily for feed level and clogging. We usually hand-feed our hogs. We bring the food to the animals twice a day in buckets which are dumped into wooden troughs. With hand-feeding, you need to clean out each trough before you add the fresh food.

Feeding and fence-checking times are the perfect opportunity to take care of a couple of other daily chores needed in land-clearing systems. First, it helps if you remove rocks, branches, and roots as the animals dig them up. Not only does this save you considerable time after the hogs are moved to their next pen, but it also eliminates any potential injury-causing materials. Expect some help from the porkers, as they think this is a game you are playing with them.

Second, watch each pig carefully for signs of illness. Be particularly alert for lack of appetite, loss of energy (the animal stays in its bed all day), and leg injuries. We also check the "manure corner" for any indications that any of the animals has diarrhea. If you spot a sick pig, you might try isolating him in a separate pen. Then refer to chapter 7 for suggestions about seeking medical help.

A final chore that you should be aware of in land-clearing operations is planning and preparing the hogs' next pen. Chapter 4 gives you the specifics on the 2-pen system. Just remember that it is better to have a second pen fenced and ready too early than too late. Never let your hogs stay in a land-clearing pen that is belly-deep with mud.

WHAT'S FOR DINNER? FEEDING YOUR PIGS

Now that your plump little porkers are all snug in their new home and you have an idea about what will be required in terms of day-to-day management, the next question that must be answered is what's the best way and best ingredients to feed them for fast growth and lean, nutritious meat?

Because approximately 60 to 70 percent of the cost to produce a pound of pork is feed and because you will be putting about 700 pounds of feed into your animal from weaner size to butcher, it's important to give this matter serious consideration. Further, the quality of the meat is determined by the quality of the feed. If the nutrition isn't in the feed, it won't be in the meat. Garbage in, garbage out. Skimping to save money will result in slower growth and low-quality pork. A balanced diet is more productive.

A Hog Nutrition Primer

More closely than any other meat-producing livestock animal, the nutritional needs of hogs parallel the dietary needs of man. In fact, they would do well on the average, well-balanced human diet. Our salivas both contain similar digestive enzymes to break starches down to sugars; we both have simple, single-chambered stomachs; our small intestines absorb nutrients into the blood via enzymes from the pancreas and bile from the gall bladder; and our large intestines absorb water (if this absorption is hindered, we both will get diarrhea). These facts should make understanding the pig's food requirements a little easier.

Hogs, like humans, are omnivores. That is, they and we benefit from both vegetable and animal food sources. A variety of ingredients in their diet, such as grains, fruits, vegetables, green forage, milk and milk by-products, eggs, and kitchen scraps, is almost certain to be successful.

Although the details of hog nutrition are too complicated to be of practical value for the average, small-scale, 2- or 3-hog operation, a little background will help you appreciate your animals and their needs. Hogs need over 35 identified, individual nutrients, which vary with age and stage of life. These include at least 12 minerals and at least 13 vitamins. The diet should include protein, carbohydrates, fats, and water. The minimum nutrient requirements are based on the National Research Council's recommendations using fed under experimental conditions with normal health and performance. These minumum values are used when preparing commerical rations.

A pig's feed requirements change from day to day and growth period to growth period. Some factors that influence an individual pig's nutrient requirements are breed, sex, and genetic background; environment, such as temperature and housing; health, condition, temperament, and amount of stress; feed quality and quantity; and absorption and availability of nutrients. Further, many other nutritional needs and factors probably haven't been identified yet, although more are being discovered almost daily.

The raiser must understand, anticipate, and be able to interpret a hog's changeable nutritional requirements. Then, feeding needs must be met. No book or set of instructions can substitute for livestock intuition, experience, skill, and good judgment where feeding is concerned.

WHAT HOGS NEED IN THEIR FEED

Although their specific nutritional needs may change over time, all hogs must have these elements in their daily diets: clean drinking water, carbohydrates for energy, protein for tissue growth and maintenance, and vitamins and minerals.

Water

The most important, most easily overlooked, and cheapest element in a hog's diet and absolutely necessary for hog health and good growth is clean water. Fifty percent or more of the animal's live weight is water. Pigs need up to 3 times as much water as dry feed every day for proper digestion. If a hog drinks less, it will eat less and convert the feed slowly, which will lead to very poor growth rates. Most hogs will drink 2 to 7 gallons of water a day per 100 pounds of body weight, and even more in hot weather.

Because leftover feed from a pig's mouth can be washed into a trough or mudhole to sour and grow bacteria, on-demand water "fountains" are generally preferred by large raisers. For the small-scale operation, an old washtub or livestock trough will suffice if you rinse and refill daily. Don't add clean water to what is already there. Also, be prepared for the inevitable overturned trough or an occasional swimming pig during the hot summer months. If you keep the trough filled with clean water, it will be harder to overturn.

Grains Provide Energy

Grains, most commonly corn, are the chief source of carbohydrates for calories and energy in hog rations. Other grains, such as barley, wheat, and grain sorghum, can be used. Oats have too much fiber for finishing, and most hogs don't like rye. A mixture of grains is generally preferred by most hogs and their raisers, although many continue to use only corn as their feed base. One word of warning about grains: Avoid spoiled grain even if you can get it free. Pigs are very sensitive to the toxins in moldy grain.

Protein Supplements

Grains alone, even expensive, improved wheat varieties, are deficient in needed protein, vitamins, and minerals. Low protein levels are responsible for slow gains and more fat than lean in the meat. A 14 to 15 percent protein level is adequate for the entire growing-finishing period, although higher levels (up to 18 percent) are often preferred for younger pigs up to 100 pounds and lower levels (down to 12 percent) for 170 pounds to market weight. Grain alone does not provide these levels, and the protein contained is not in a form usable (incomplete) by the pig's body. Hence, protein supplements are added to the grain feed.

The most popular commercially used protein source is soybean oil meal. High in usable protein and readily available as a by-product of the soybean oil industry, soybean oil meal can be purchased from feed suppliers as a concentrate for self-feeders and mix-your-own diets. It is also a common additive in prepared rations.

Many raisers supplement protein with milk and dairy products, such as whey, cottage cheese, yogurt, and skim milk powder. Feeding hogs milk also seems to aid in the control of internal parasites, although we don't know how or why. A gallon or a gallon and a half a day per hog supplies all the necessary protein and is an especially good practice on farms where milk is in surplus during the hog-raising months. Famous Danish pork is milk-fed. One more point for milk: pigs love it. Rarely will milk-soaked grain be left to sour in the trough.

Grazing on good legume pasture also aids in meeting the protein requirements of pigs that weigh more than 75 pounds. Younger pigs can't digest the forage as well, and some may even develop intestinal problems from the high fiber content of pasture grasses. If you plan to raise your hogs on pasture, you may need to confine your weaner pigs to a small pen for a few weeks to limit their fiber intake. Otherwise, monitor your feed ingredients to control fiber intake in growing pigs weighing under 75 pounds.

One more alternative for protein supplementing is eggs, another hog favorite that is a common farm surplus item. Up to a dozen eggs, shells and all, per day per hog will meet their protein requirement. Further, the minerals in the shells, especially calcium, also are beneficial.

Some excellent protein sources such as nuts, seeds, cooked soybeans, and fish products may be very tasty to the hogs but shouldn't be fed during the final 2 months before butchering. The unsaturated, liquid fats contained in these food products will cause *soft pork*, meat that remains soft, flabby, and oily even after refrigeration. Soft pork is virtually impossible to slice into bacon and other thin cuts and is rated unusable by pork processors. According to most experts, the fat in a hog requires at least 4 to 6 weeks to change from soft to firm. Hence, protein sources which tend to cause soft pork can be used only up to the final 2 months of feeding without causing any problems.

Two of the above protein feeds, soybeans and sunflower seeds, need further warnings. Raw soybeans contain a digestive enzyme inhibitor which is deactivated by heat. Hogs and humans alike should eat only cooked soybeans because raw ones may reduce protein absorption. Sunflower seeds, especially unshelled seeds, have a high fiber content and have been shown to have limited use with swine, especially young animals, although some experts suggest they can be used for up to 50 percent of the diet of older hogs.

Vitamins and Minerals

Grain feed also must be supplemented to add sufficient vitamins and minerals to the diet. Although pigs, unlike humans, produce their own vitamin C, their diets are commonly deficient in vitamins A, D, E, K, B-series, iron, calcium, and phosphorus. When pigs are raised on pasture or in clearing lots, they tend to get most if not all of these requirements from the plants, the soil, and the sun. However, hogs raised on concrete, especially those in confinement, will suffer from a wide variety of nutritional deficiency diseases unless care is taken with their diet.

One way to add vitamins and minerals is the old practice of giving hogs clean sod to root in and eat. This was the way our grandfathers prevented iron deficiency anemia in baby pigs before the availability of oral and injected iron supplements. However, digging up and carrying clean sod to the pigpen on a daily basis is labor intensive, to say the least.

Most commercial raisers find it easier and less of a bother to add a vitamin/mineral premix to their grain or feed it free choice. One warning with free-choice vitamins/minerals: Most have toxic levels if overeaten and many are destroyed by heat and moisture if they sit in the feeder too long. Although pigs are usually fairly wise about how much additive to consume, occasionally one will find something unresistably tasty and overeat to the point of illness.

Pigs also need salt (sodium chloride) in their diets, up to 0.25 percent of the feed. Salt, like other additives, can be toxic at levels above 2 percent—especially if inadequate water is available.

Fat

The diet of a growing pig should contain limited fat, no more than 10 percent. A diet richer than this will result in a fatty carcass and pork cuts with thick fat bands.

Table 6–1 gives a general overview of the nutrients hogs need in their daily menu.

Table 6-1

A HOG'S BASE FEEDING NEEDS

Feed Element	Amount
WATER:	2–7 gallons per day per 100 pounds (minimum)
GRAINS (energy):	75–90% of total feed ration
PROTEIN:	14–15% of ration for growing/finishing period 16–18% for growing pigs under 100 pounds 12–14% for finishing hogs over 170 pounds
VITAMINS/ MINERALS:	Usually provided as a mix or by access to pasture grasses, roots, soil, sunshine. Need A, D, E, K, B-series and other vitamins Need iron, calcium, phosphorus, and other minerals
SALT:	0.25% of feed ration maximum (over 2% is toxic)
FAT:	10% of ration maximum

Table 6–1. General overview of daily nutritional requirements of hogs.

HOW MUCH DOES AN AVERAGE GROWING PIG EAT?

Although variations occur based on the animal's activity level and other factors, these guidelines are relatively accurate: A 30-pound pig will eat 2 pounds and gain 1 pound a day; 45 days later, he should weigh about 100 pounds and be eating 3 to 4 pounds and gaining 2 pounds a day; in another month and a half, he will weigh about 200 pounds and be eating 4 or more pounds and gaining over 2 pounds a day. If the feed is less concentrated, he may eat twice this amount. Table 6–2 shows what you can expect from your hog in terms of feed consumption and growth.

Keep in mind that pastured pigs will eat up to 20 percent less grain and up to 50 percent less protein supplement, according to some sources, and may make slower gains than less-active animals.

Table 6-2

SWINE EXPECTANCY TABLE

	Growing Pigs				Finishing Pigs		Total or Average for Period
Live Weight Range (lbs.)	10-25	25-50	50-75	75-125	125-175	175-225	215
Expected Average Gain/Day (lbs.)	0.6	1.1	1.3	1.6	1.8	1.9	1.4
Av. Daily Air-Dry Feed* Consumption (lbs.)	0.5	2.4	3.5	4.8	6.2	7.2	4.2
Total Feed Required for Period (lbs.)	12	55	65	148	172	187	640
Av. Feed Conversion (lbs.)	1.2	2.2	2.6	2.9	3.4	3.7	3.0
No. Days in Period	25	23	19	31	28	26	152

*Figures based on air dry basis, commercial complete ration.

Table 6-2. The above figures are based on baby pigs nursing until they weigh 40 to 50 pounds. Feed is in pellet form. Similar feed in mash form will result in conversion rates that are about 10 percent lower. (From: Cenex Hog Feeding and Management Guide.)

On the average, hogs will consume 3 to 5 pounds of food per pig per day during the growing period (when the pig weighs 40 to 125 pounds) and 5 to 7.5 pounds per pig per day during the finishing period (when the pig weighs 125 to 220 pounds). Most raisers consider "full feeding" to be based on 4 to 6 pounds of complete ration per 100 pounds live weight of hog.

Beware of overfeeding your hogs. Unfortunately, some pigs have a tendency to overeat if the food is available. The result is considerable leftover and wasted feed and possibly even digestive disturbances and diarrhea. Furthermore, overeating does not result in faster growth, and it may result in a fattier carcass.

Compare your hogs' ration consumption to what is expected for their age group. If you find that your hogs are demanding far too much hand-fed rations, or they are emptying the self-feeder too fast, cut back their daily feed amount a little bit each day. Don't let them bully you into overfeeding (some hogs get downright dictatorial). You might even want to consider a limited feeding program.

Some raisers claim that limiting feed after the hogs reach 125 pounds usually improves feed efficiency and carcass quality. However, this program may require up to an extra month for the animal to reach butcher weight.

Table 6-3

DAILY GAIN AND DAYS TO BUTCHER WEIGHT

Starting Weight	Expected Daily Gain	Days to 220 Pounds
pounds	pounds	days
30	1.35	140
40	1.40	130
50	1.50	115
60	1.55	105
70	1.55	100
80	1.55	90
90	1.60	85
100	1.60	75

(From: Washington State University Cooperative Extension Service, Pork Industry Handbook #1036, March 1982.)

Table 6-3. These figures show an average daily gain and days to butcher weight (220 pounds) for good quality pigs properly fed.

To limit feed, the hogs must be fed individually or in very small groups in order to monitor how much feed is being consumed per animal. They are given 70 to 90 percent of full feed (1 pound feed per 30 pounds weight of hog) or only what the animal will consume in 20 to 30 minutes. Extra food is removed.

Limited feeding can be managed easily in confinement situations where the entire diet is controlled by the raiser. However, we've found that pastured and clearing-lot hogs tend to compensate for the decreased grain-based diet by more actively seeking alternate food sources such as vegetation, roots, and earthworms.

EXPECTED GROWTH PATTERNS

Most small-scale pork producers want to know how long they should be prepared to feed their hogs before the pigs are big enough to butcher. Further, they want to know what to consider an average daily growth pattern. Table 6–3 breaks down when you can expect your hogs to reach market or butchering size if you feed them a proper diet.

THE EASIEST WAY TO FEED: BY THE SACK

Most commercial rations already contain protein, salt, limited fat, and the identified vitamins and minerals hogs need. Although this is the most expensive way to raise pork, feeding an already formulated diet takes away much of the guesswork and eliminates nearly all of the labor preparing feed. Some raisers claim that feeding commercially prepared diets takes advantage of modern nutrition science, which dates back to the 1920s. Further, if a large number of swine are being grown, commercial rations are often profitable. With one or two pigs, however, using a totally purchased diet adds considerably to the pork production costs. You may still come out ahead on the price of pork per pound (if you compare your homegrown price per pound using a purchased ration to retail pork price per pound), but it will be close.

Watch Out: Many commercial formulas contain additives such as antibiotics (biological compounds that inhibit or kill microorganisms), chemotherapeutics (chemicals that act like antibiotics), and anthelmintics (dewormers). These ingredients are not needed by the small-scale raiser.

Antibiotics and chemotherapeutics are routinely added to "starter" rations for very young pigs. Used in the United States for more than 25 years, these additives reduce mortality by preventing diseases usually found in crowded confinement operations. They also act as a growth stimulant resulting in a 10 percent increase in feed efficiency. However, limited disease problems on the small-scale do not require routine medication in the feed, and concerns about bacterial resistance, reduced natural immunity, and drug residues in the animal tissue have surfaced recently.

If one of your reasons for raising your own pork is to avoid commercial additives, such as antibiotics, read the feed tag before purchasing and ask questions if you don't understand the terms.

MILLER LIVESTOCK CO., INC. 107

Net Weight 80 lbs. (36.2 KG.)

SWINE GROWER — 16

GUARANTEED ANALYSIS

Min. Cr. Protein	16.0%
Min. Cr. Fat	6.0%
Max. Cr. Fiber	7.0%
Moisture, not more than	10.0%

Made from: Corn, Raypro (single cell protein), Processed Grain by products, Cane Molasses, Limestone, Monocalcium Phosphate, Dicalcium Phosphate, Brewer's Yeast, Salt, Manganese, Zinc, Iron, Copper, Iodine, Cobalt, Selenium, Vitamin A, Vitamin D-3, Vitamin E, Vitamin K (MSBC), Vitamin B-12, Riboflavin, Pantothenic Acid, Niacin, Choline Chloride, and Ethoxyquin.

Swine Grower — 16 may be fed as a complete feed to pigs from 40 lbs. body weight to 150 lbs. body weight. Clean water should be available to the animals at all times.

manufactured by

MILLER LIVESTOCK COMPANY, INC.

107 Graham, WA 98338
(206) 847-2919

What you can expect to find on a feed tag.

Most feedstore diets are either ground (coarsely or finely) into a "dry mash" or pelletized. Grinding consists of breaking the hard grain kernels into smaller, more uniform particles. Dry mash is often powdery with lots of dust. Finely ground feed is best for very young pigs, while older hogs do better on a medium to coarse grind. However, many pigs find powdery feed unpalatable in any case.

We've found that ground rations work best as a liquid or paste feed. Hogs seem to perform better on a feed/water mixture; scientists have found that they eat more and grow faster. Milk and eggs can replace part of the water. Although the liquid in the food reduces the need for supplemental water, clean water should still be available at all times. Despite improved hog performance, the wet-mash method is not used commercially because it requires too much labor (mixing and feeding) or expensive equipment (mixing vats, holding tanks, and pumps) to feed it automatically.

Our pigs love a mash made with ground rations and hot water or warm milk on a cold morning. However, they get spoiled easily with this hot cereal breakfast!

If you use the wet mash mixture, be sure to wash out all the buckets used to transport the mixture to the pen and wash the troughs between feedings. Wet grain sours in short order and may contaminate future batches of feed.

Pelletized feeds, although more expensive than ground feeds, are popular because there is reduced dust, less storage space is required, and less feed is wasted by the pigs. The pellets are formed by steaming fine or medium ground feed and then extruding it through a die. The length, diameter, and hardness are variable. Young pigs don't like overly hard pellets, but most pigs will prefer pellets to dry meal if given a choice. We've found that our hogs are equally fond of either pellets or a wet mash mixture or a mixture of both.

Commercial, balanced feed rations can be purchased in 80-pound bags or in bulk quantities. We save considerable costs per pound of feed (up to 25 percent) by purchasing it in bulk (usually by the pound, but occasionally by the ton), supplying our own containers. You can calculate how much you will need by referring to Table 6–2.

If you intend to purchase a 5-month or 6-month supply of ration at one time, you will need several clean 55-gallon drums or other suitable containers with tight-fitting lids. Keep the feed storage area clean (sweep up spilled feed immediately) and the containers covered, or you may be inviting rodent trouble.

THE OTHER WAY: BALANCING YOUR OWN HOG DIET

If you want to produce your homegrown pork as cheaply as possible, the best way to do it is with homegrown feed. Your labor costs, especially if you grow all the feed components, will skyrocket, but out-of-pocket cash expenditures will decline.

The basic principles of ration balancing are very similar to those you use when balancing your own diet: Carbohydrates, protein, and vitamins/minerals are all needed for growth and health. Garden and field produce such as corn, root crops, squash, fruits, and pasture legumes supplemented with protein sources, such as milk and eggs, provide all the nutrition a hog needs.

Grains or Peas Form Ration Base

Like commercial rations, corn and other grains are the feed base, providing carbohydrates and other lesser nutrients. Corn is a fairly easy grain to raise on a small scale. It yields more than twice as many bushels per acre as other cereal grains and has become the standard feed for hogs, especially in the Midwest. Wheat is actually a better feed with a higher protein content, but it is more expensive to grow on a small scale, requiring expensive harvest machinery or labor-intensive hand harvesting methods.

All grains must be dried and put through a grinder before a hog can digest them. When whole grains are fed, much will come through the pig's intestines unchanged. Unless you already have the equipment, drying and grinding your own grains is an expensive proposition. Sometimes you can find a custom processor to do it for you. Use a medium grind screen, ¼ to ½ inch, for general purpose feeding. Young pigs might do better with a finer grind (⅛ to 3/16 inch) and older hogs with a coarser grind (over ½ inch).

Pacific Northwest swine scientists have found that dry cull peas (the small, shriveled, cracked, and otherwise damaged seeds not suited for human food as split peas in the commercial pea industry) are a good homegrown feed base in parts of the country where peas grow better than corn. Although lower in energy than grains, peas are an excellent protein source, lowering the need to supplement by one-half. Further, pigs over 10 weeks of age seem to like peas, fresh or dried, raw or cooked (grains mix better with raw or dried peas).

Peas are not good enough for a complete diet, however, as they are low in calcium, selenium, and vitamin E. Nonetheless, many small farmers may find them to be the perfect base for their hog ration.

Supplements to the Ration Base

Some raisers suggest that comfrey is an excellent homegrown supplement for hogs. Jerome Belanger, author of *The Homestead Hog*, was the first to publish this idea. Comfrey is the only land plant which contains vitamin B$_{12}$, a nutrient that reduces the pig's protein requirement. Further, pigs like comfrey, it is easy to grow by root expansion, and it has a protein content comparable to clover, though not quite as high as alfalfa.

Pigs love pumpkin. In fact, it is the major hog food in China. Actually, pigs like just about all vine crops that humans do, including squashes of all kinds, melons, and even tomatoes.

Swine can also take an active part in your fruit harvest, as they relish the excess from orchards, vines, and bushes. Pigs even like the old, bruised, rotting fruit. We once gave our hogs a barrel of waste apples left over after squeezing cider. However, the fruit at the bottom of the container had begun to ferment. Although our porkers loved it, they seemed to stagger a bit that day—and they slept a little sounder that night!

Root crops, such as Jerusalem artichokes, potatoes, rutabagas, turnips, carrots, and beets, are also excellent for pigs. The porkers will harvest their own if set loose for a few hours in the field. Root-feeding like this is still used extensively in northern Europe. However, root crop production on a large scale requires much hand labor or expensive planting and harvesting equipment. Also, the crops are not easy to store and feed. Therefore, most hog raisers agree that root crop feeding probably should be limited to garden surplus, no more than a third of the diet, to be economical from a feed and labor perspective.

Speaking of the garden, raising pigs and gardens at the same time of the year is an excellent example of *symbiosis*, working together. The pigs get the thinnings, surplus, and harvest waste (which satisfy most if not all of their vitamin requirements) which lessens the feed bill. We recommend that you plant a little extra corn, peas, and vine and root crops when you are raising summer hogs. However, because pigs like just about the same garden and orchard produce that you do, feel free to experiment. And don't worry if the zucchini outproduces itself or the apple trees have a particularly good year; with hogs on the farm, nothing edible goes to waste!

However, be aware that ration balancing is a complex skill to master. We feel safer using a complete commercial ration (formulated by swine scientists who know far more about a hog's dietary needs than we do) and supplementing, free choice, with vegetation, roots, and soil goodies; garden, dairy, and egg surpluses; and, kitchen wastes when they are available. This way, we know our hogs are getting all their nutrition via their purchased feed. The home-grown extras give them some variety, extra vitamins, and we usually need to feed less of the purchased ration. We recommend that you use a complete commercial ration as your feed base, too, especially when you are just starting out with hogs.

If you want to try a completely homegrown diet, however, your local agricultural extension agent can help you with your questions about using homegrown hog rations. Use a little common sense and "think like a pig" who eats remarkably like a human and you should have no problems.

WHAT ABOUT FEEDING HOGS GARBAGE?

So, you surmise, if pigs do well on human food, why not just feed human leftovers? Because, to be frank, it is illegal. Several major swine diseases, some transferable to humans, such as trichinosis, have been traced to feeding hogs waste. Therefore, the law requires that all garbage fed to pigs be cooked for at least 30 minutes at 212 degrees F. before feeding. This results in an homogeneous, uniformly colored, and textured soupy mixture that is actually preferred for hog feeding since it prevents the hogs from picking out the goodies and leaving the rest. Needless to say, this cooking requires large vats made specifically for the purpose, especially if you raise more than just a couple of hogs.

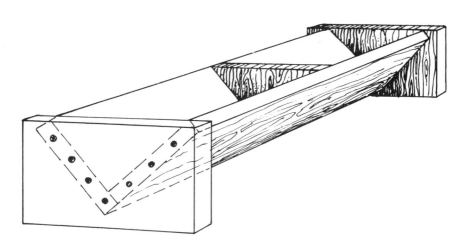

A simple "V" trough made from 2 planks with boards nailed over the ends.

Kitchen scraps and garden waste do not fall into the classification of garbage. For legal purposes, "garbage" is the waste collected from restaurants, military bases, hospitals, and other large-scale feeding operations. Household leftovers can be fed uncooked if they contain no raw meat scraps. Actually, this practice solves a disposal problem and can reduce feed costs to some extent. Much of what would normally go into the compost pile can go into your porkers. Just beware of feeding any wastes and garbage that isn't produced in your own kitchen.

FEEDING: WHERE AND HOW?

Besides the question of what to feed, you must consider ways to feed. Oh, yes, there is more to "slopping the hogs" than simply tossing a bucket of food into their pen. For profitable pork, it is desirable to find the most economical feeding method in terms of equipment and labor to achieve the lowest cost per unit of gain.

Hand-Feeding

Hand-fed hogs have their feed brought to them twice a day and placed in feeding troughs which are normally located near the shelter. A simple "V" trough, as illustrated, is common and works well. Allow at least 12 to 18 inches of trough length per pig. A feed trough takes a lot of abuse, so use heavy planks and large nails, and be sure that your construction is sound.

Large hogs may amuse themselves by tossing their feeders around after they have cleaned them out, but if you use sturdy wood and plenty of nails, they won't do much damage. Some pigs enjoy walking in their feed or snoozing in their empty troughs. Crossbars will prevent these habits, and they will also divide up the feeding area to lessen the amount of squabbling over choice tidbits.

If you are concerned that the feeding area will become muddy or if it bothers you that playtime consists of moving your carefully constructed troughs around the pen, try anchoring the feeders on heavy planks or to a concrete feeding area. We won't guarantee that this will work—pigs are pretty resourceful and somehow manage to move the trough no matter how well you nail it down. Also, we've found that trough moving is beneficial in a way; it keeps spilled food from building up under and around the trough, hence lessening spoilage odors and rodent problems.

There are 2 main disadvantages to hand-feeding hogs. First, it requires daily labor. You have to take the feed to the pigs at least twice a day and there is no getting out of it. If you are an hour or two late with dinner, your porcine pals will know and they'll let you know that they know. Second, you are responsible for balancing the

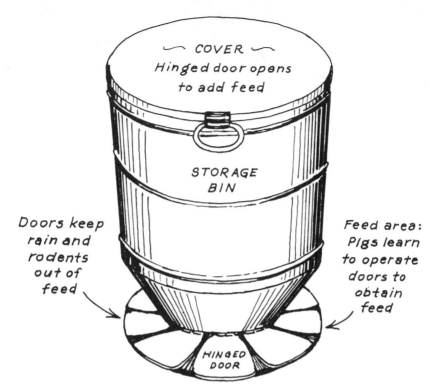

A commercial, on-demand self-feeder can hold up to several weeks worth of dry food. This model is available in many sizes, generally made of metal

diet since they have no opportunity to balance it for themselves (except with the nutrition gleaned from available vegetation and soil). Hence, be sure that the meals you serve are nutritional.

Some raisers hand-feed their hogs 3 or 4 times a day which approximates how a self-fed hog eats (a little here, a little there). However twice a day, morning and evening (during warm weather, hogs eat better if fed in the cool parts of the day), is sufficient. Because hogs learn to anticipate feeding times, regularity is very important to avoid undue stress.

Yes, hand-feeding has it's advantages, too. Equipment-wise, it is very inexpensive. All you need is a trough and a bucket. Also, hand-feeding forces you to visit with your hogs at least twice daily. These are the perfect opportunities to watch for signs of illness or other problems on a regular basis. Don't be surprised if you even enjoy these times together.

Self-Feeding

The second, and probably the most popular, method of feeding hogs is the self-feeding way. "Ad lib" feeding and watering systems date back to 1677. Using special storage-release feeders, food is available to the hogs at all times. Hinged doors can be opened by the pig and also serve to keep out rodents and rain. Experts agree that you should allow no more than 4 pigs per self-feeder "hole" to prevent fighting over feed.

Self-feeders have a tendency to clog. Most have some way to agitate the feed to keep it from forming "bridges." They also have adjustable "throats" (the section between storage tank and feeder) for controlling the rate of flow.

Self-feeders are either placed on concrete or wood plank platforms to prevent mudholes from appearing around the base in wet weather.

With self-feeding, you have the option of purchasing or mixing a complete menu, or giving the hogs access to all the components of a balanced menu in different feeders and then letting them balance their own feed. As you can probably guess, self-feeders are designed only for a dry ration, pelleted or mash type, which is what you purchase commercially. If you plan to use homegrown feed, you must either dry and grind it before placing it in the self-feeder, or you must use troughs and hand-feeding. Wet mash feeding is suitable only for hand-feeding with troughs.

Self-feeders are popular with large-scale raisers. The pigs quickly learn to lift the hinged doors to get at the feed.

The method of self-feeding most common with large-scale raisers is to offer grain in one feeder, a protein supplement in another, salt/minerals in a third, etc. Given this opportunity, most hogs are fairly adept at creating a nutritious diet. Some, however, will find one component more palatable (usually the protein) and will "pig out" at that feeder, limiting access by other pigs, wasting expensive supplements, and possibly getting sick from the toxic effects of too many vitamins and minerals. Also, pigs have been known to overeat and get too fat when fed on demand. Keep a daily check on your hogs' food intake.

The biggest advantage of self-feeding is that it's easy. If you have a large storage feeder and only a couple of pigs, several weeks worth of food can be made available. Also, the hogs learn early that food is always available,so they are less likely to eat too fast (which can cause digestive disturbances) or fight over feed. They learn to eat a little here and a little there at their leisure.

However, on-demand feeders have a few disadvantages, too. They are expensive—although they usually last for many years. Additionally, they must be checked daily for clogging. Also, you can tend to ignore what's going on in the pigpen if you only need to fill the feeder occasionally. Pigs have been known to get sick and even die before the raiser notices. Daily observation is important no matter which feeding method you select.

The only concluding remark we would like to make is a reminder: Don't forget to supply clean, fresh water daily—no matter which feeding methods or rations you select. We use a galvanized water trough which we clean and refill daily. A smaller container, such as a roasting pan, may be sufficient when the piglets are small. Large-scale hog producers prefer automatic watering equipment composed of a pressurized pumping system which connects to individualized drinking nipples or lever-controlled basins. As with most hog-raising equipment, the automated waterers are much more expensive than hand-operated systems and like self-feeders, the self-waterers are prone to clogging and need to be checked daily.

Now you should be all ready to go. If you need more information about hog feeds and feeding, again we will refer you to your agricultural extension agent or a neighboring hog farmer.

Chapter 7

TROUBLESHOOTING

Unless you are luckier than 99.9 percent of hog raisers, expect to have some trouble with your porkers from time to time. It happens to all of us. "Be prepared for the worst" is the best advice we can give.

HELP! MY PIGS ARE LOOSE!

It will probably happen at least once. You look out of the window and there's your prize porker digging up your garden, wandering down the driveway, or curiously sniffing your best roses. Don't panic! Nothing will lessen your chances of retrieving Porky faster than screaming, running, chasing, and flailing about in a panic-stricken furor.

If you've had the pigs for a few weeks or longer, chances are they know you and they probably know the dinner bucket, too.

Calmly and with a cool head, go outside and try calling the pigs by name (if they have names). Contrary to popular opinion, pigs are as smart as dogs and can be taught to come when called—especially if they think you have food. If direct calling doesn't seem to move them toward you, get a bucket of corn or dry pelletized feed and shake it loudly while continuing to call. This almost always works, and the pigs will follow the rattling food back into the pen. As you might expect, nothing attracts a curious hog faster than dinner.

Some pig experts suggest moving a pig backwards with a bucket or basket over its head, using the tail like a steering wheel. We've never seen this work. However, we do have a friend who ties a rope to the hog's back leg and walks it backwards to the destination. He says this works great and the only hard part is getting the rope onto the leg.

Many feed stores and livestock supply houses sell pig snares or "hog holders." These look like a rope noose on a metal bar. The idea is to slip the noose over the hog's snout, behind the biggest teeth, and pull the rope tight. Then, supposedly, you can convince the pig to follow you wherever you want him to go. Again, we've never seen this work.

If all else fails to entice your animals back to their pen, try picking up a board, a piece of plywood, or a "hurdle" (a large, thick piece of board with a handle for moving animals) to use as a guiding fence. Then, walk your pig slowly back toward the enclosure. Don't rush the animal; let him walk at his own pace and stay to his rear. If assistance is available, have everyone do the same thing. This way, no matter which way the pig turns, someone will be blocking him from heading in the wrong direction.

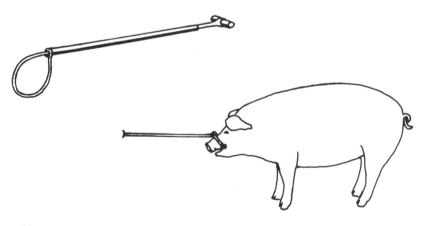

Pig snares.

Never use electric prods to move pigs because severe injuries, including stress-related death, have been known to occur. Canvas "slappers" and whips have been used with some success to guide an unruly hog. We don't use them, however.

One thing to keep in mind is that pigs follow a leader, although not as easily as sheep or cattle. Nonetheless, if you can convince one animal to return home, the odds are good that any other escapees will follow suit—especially if they think the leader gets dinner first.

One of these solutions has always worked for us, and we've had our share of escaped porkers. However, if nothing seems to be doing the trick for you, our advice is to seek more experienced help—immediately!

RESTRAINING THE HOG

Restraint is a pig problem that is directly related to the problem of escapes. Pigs need to be restrained when being moved between pens or into a truck, for physical examinations, or when you are administering medications to them. But how do you convince a 200-pound animal to go where you want him to go or to hold still?

Again, be as gentle and quiet as possible. Don't frighten or chase a pig. They have very sharp teeth and can bite if they are frightened. Further, they are built low to the ground and all that bulk could knock your feet right out from under you if Porky bolts and runs in panic.

Some of the suggestions we made in the preceding section for moving an escaped pig also will be appropriate if you need to move a pig between fenced areas or from a pasture to a pen. Most raisers routinely move pigs with whips and ropes and gates and plywood sheets between them and the animals. Obviously, these folks aren't friends with their hogs and the hogs know it. Although sheets of plywood can be handy for keeping the pigs' attention focused on the desired destination, we haven't had much use for a great deal of other animal trainer equipment. But then again, we've always made friends with our animals.

We've found that moving pigs between pens or from a pen into a livestock truck is quite easy to accomplish if the porkers know a feed bucket and respond to corn or feed pellets rattling in it. So we start training our little ones as soon as we get them home to follow this dinner bell wherever we ring it. Hence, our hogs will follow that bucket of food just about anywhere. Therefore, we recommend that you, too, teach your pigs about rattling feed buckets early—you'll never have to worry about escaped pigs or moving day.

Now there's the next problem: holding a pig still for examination or medication. Most large-scale hog raisers have special chutes designed just for this purpose. The animal is herded into a very small, fenced-in enclosure which is so limited in size that the animal cannot move or even turn around. Here, the owner or the veterinarian can perform the necessary procedures without a fight from the animal or the risk of injury to either the hog or the person.

This arrangement works well—if you have the special facilities. But what do you do if you don't?

We've found that if you want a pig to lie down and remain as if in a trance for examinations or medication, there's an easier, more reliable way than ropes and brute strength or special pens. Try a belly rub. We haven't seen a pig yet who didn't lie down on his back and go into a sleep-like state when his belly was rubbed. They love it. And it's fun to do even when restraint isn't the issue.

HOW CAN I TELL HOW MUCH MY PIG WEIGHS?

How do you know when Porky is ready for market if you aren't adept at estimating weight by just looking him over, and you don't use floor scales like large hog-raising operations? The best way we've found is to calculate weight by body measurement.

But how does one measure a pig, you ask? True, it's not always easy. Most of the time, Porky thinks it's a game and will grab one end of the measuring tape or try to wrap it around your legs.

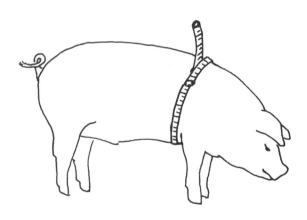

Wrap the measuring tape just behind the front legs to get the "heart girth" measurement.

If you have a restraint enclosure, this is a good place for performing measurements. Or you can find a helper who will play the "belly rubber." Once the pig is in the restraining pen or laying down and entranced, wrap a standard measuring tape (the kind you buy at any sewing supplies store) around the pig, just behind the front legs, to get the "heart girth" measurement. Then, measure the animal's length down the backbone from ears to tail.

Your basic calculation is:

$$\frac{[heart\ girth] \times [heart\ girth] \times [length]}{400}$$

Believe it or not, that will equal the animal's weight in pounds. This method is accurate within 3 percentage points of the hog's actual weight. Some raisers suggest adding 7 extra pounds if the pig weighs less than 150 pounds by this calculation to get a more accurate weight.

HELP! MY PIG IS SICK!

Hog diseases are often difficult to diagnose, even for the experienced. Many illnesses have the same symptoms and some have no symptoms at all, but the pork may be affected. Luckily, disease is rarely a problem for the small-scale raiser as many illnesses most frequently are caused by predisposing factors (stress, overcrowding, etc.) not found on the small farm.

Prevention is more important than treatment. Start with healthy stock from healthy farms; provide proper housing, nutrition, and sanitation; remove manure regularly; watch the pigs on a daily basis for irregularities and changes in habit; and clean all pens thoroughly between pigs (elbow grease and sunshine are the best disinfectants).

Despite the excellent odds in your favor, you still may find yourself with a disease problem. Don't try to deal with it yourself. All hog diseases require trained help to diagnose and treat. Sure it costs money to have the vet come out and take a look, but if you don't know what you are fighting, you can lose a hog. Further, you'll probably need advice and assistance in selecting and administering medications.

The disease descriptions in this chapter are meant only for your information and understanding. The discussion should help you realize when and why veterinary services are necessary. We do not recommend that disease descriptions in this book be used as diagnostic and treatment tools unless you live so far out in the sticks that the animal could die before help arrives — and even in that case, you should probably consult with a neighboring hog farmer before proceeding with treatment yourself.

MAINTAINING HEALTHY HOGS

As the old cliché goes, an ounce of disease prevention is worth a pound of cure. Sickness and death are most frequently the problems of poorly managed, filthy, overcrowded hog lots. These raisers may figure that if they lose a hog or 2 or 3 to disease, so what? Maybe they think it would cost more to clean up their swine facilities than it would cost to lose a few pigs. However, when you are only raising 2 animals, half of your operation goes down the drain if 1 animals dies due to your neglect. Therefore, it makes sense to give your animals every opportunity to stay healthy.

Start with healthy piglets from a reputable farmer. Then, keep your pigs' living quarters cleaned. Remove the manure at least every week or two (depending on the pen size—see chapter 8 for more information on that subject); don't let the animals live in mud up to their bellies; provide protection from drafts and sun; and make sure that the bedding you use is changed regularly and kept clean.

The next step to insuring healthy hogs is a proper diet. Many pig diseases are related to or indirectly caused by nutritional deficiencies. If you don't trust yourself to mix a balanced ration from grains and other foodstuffs, buy a prepared hog mix to be assured that your animals get all the nutrients they need.

Some hog raisers, especially those raising many animals in close confinement, routinely feed antibiotics to their swine to lessen the chances of disease. We don't recommend that the small-scale raiser resort to this option. In fact, many questions have been asked recently regarding this practice as antibiotic-resistant bacterial strains have been discovered, as well as antibiotic residues in the meat from these animals. Feeding animals medications will not prevent any disease that you can't prevent with proper management.

A constant supply of fresh, clean water is important for healthy animals. Wash the water container (if you use one) thoroughly each time you change the water. Don't let dirt and scum build up.

Rid your pig facilities of disease-carrying rodents and keep food stored securely so that rats are not attracted to the area.

Get to know your hog-raising neighbors and local large-animal veterinarians. Find out which diseases are common in your area, and what symptoms they produce. Get some opinions about which vaccinations or routine procedures, such as worming and dusting for skin parasites, might be needed in your area. One day, when you least expect it, you may need to call on a more experienced farmer or doctor for advice and assistance. It always helps to develop a working relationship before an emergency strikes.

RECOGNIZING DISEASE

Make a habit of closely observing your pigs on a daily basis so you will know immediately when one isn't feeling well. He may remain in his bed and refuse to eat or stagger or cough or sneeze. Other problems such as abnormal temperature, inflammation, and swellings won't always be as easy to spot.

When you suspect illness, look for symptoms such as nasal discharge, coughing, labored breathing, diarrhea, constipation, a bleeding or infected wound, or bumps and lumps. Observe the animal's behavior and outward appearance for as long as it takes to get a complete picture of his condition.

Next, you will need to get an accurate reading of the animal's body temperature. Taking a hog's temperature may not be easy, but it is almost always an essential diagnostic tool. A pig's normal temperature range is 101.6 to 103.6 degrees F. Hot weather and excitement may increase it somewhat without disease being present.

To take a pig's temperature, first relax the animal with a belly rub, even if he is already laying down from illness. We've found that a soothing rub along with some quiet talk convinces the ill pig that you mean no harm and you are there to help. Then, when the hog is calm and quiet, carefully and slowly insert a well-lubricated (use petroleum jelly or something similar) rectal thermometer (the regular human type found at all drugstores) with a string attached so you can retrieve it if necessary. Leave the thermometer in the rectal cavity for at least 3 minutes before you take a reading.

If the temperature is normal, but the animal is down and not eating, the problem is probably digestive, metabolic, or a functional disorder. Check the hog's diet to make sure he is getting all the nutrition he needs (we've found that offering some special goodies is often enough to get the animal up and eating). Then watch him for a day or two to see if the condition improves. If the hog gets worse or fails to improve, call your veterinarian for advice and assistance.

If fever is present, it may be a viral or bacterial infection. If the fever is very high (over 105 degrees F.), it is probably a respiratory, reproductive, or urinary disease. In any case of fever, a professional opinion of the seriousness of the problem is definitely needed at once.

If the hog's temperature is well below normal, summon help immediately; subnormal body temperature means that the animal is probably close to death.

When you call your veterinarian about a sick hog, give him the symptoms and the animal's temperature. Often, the doctor will give you advice, free of charge, by phone. If it sounds like a simple infection or sickness that you can treat yourself with injected or oral antibiotics, sometimes you can pick them up at the animal hospital — complete with instructions. In other cases, the veterinarian may want to come out and take a look before making a diagnosis. If this is the case, consider the fee well spent if it means saving your animal.

Most veterinarians charge a flat rate per hour to come to a farm (most do not have the facilities for you to bring the animals to them, like you might with a dog or a cat). Some add a mileage rate. Of course, you will pay extra for any necessary medications. If money is a problem, many veterinarians will let you make payments, and some will even trade their services for something of equal value. The doctor is concerned, just like you, with restoring the health of your animal and will make every effort to work out a financial arrangement that you can afford. If the choice is between saving a buck by treating something life-threatening yourself and calling in a professional, spend the money.

The bottom line is this: confirm all disease suspicions with a professional diagnosis. Needless to say, we will not be recommending any home remedies or telling you ways to shortcut doctor bills. In fact, we are on a first-name basis with 2 local large-animal doctors, and we have no reservations about calling them for advice. Although we've been extremely fortunate and have had few disease problems with our animals, we are prepared for the worst. We suggest that you educate yourself with the following disease information, call your local veterinarians for their advice, and remember that a nutritious diet, proper housing, and lack of stress are as important when treating diseases as they are for preventing them.

DICTIONARY OF DISEASES

Abscesses. An infection of wounds and internal organs usually caused by a strain of *Streptococcus* bacteria. An abscess is a walled-off collection of living and dead bacteria, dead cells, and body fluids (this collection is commonly called "pus") that can occur anywhere in the body. Symptoms include high fever, reduced feed intake, constipation, and pain. It is treated by surgically draining the abscess if possible and using local, injected and oral antibiotics.

You can treat an abscess yourself (lance the wound and clean out the pus) if the abscess is accessible (not on an internal organ) and if you are sure what you are treating is indeed an abscess (ask for a professional opinion if you are not certain). We recommend that a doctor perform this operation, however.

Anemia. Usually anemia occurs in baby pigs from a deficiency of iron in the sow's milk. It may also be caused by deficiencies in copper, vitamin B^{12}, or vitamin E. The symptoms are weakness, lethargy, and lack of appetite. Treat with dietary supplements following a professional confirmation of the deficiency. Diet additives can be purchased from many feed stores and are also available through animal hospitals.

Arthritis. Usually caused by *mycoplasma* bacteria in young pigs who walk on hard surfaces in damp confinement conditions. Symptoms include limping and swollen, painful joints. It is often treated with corticosteroid injections after professional diagnosis.

Atrophic Rhinitis. Also known as "bull nose," this is a nasal infection caused by a bacteria, *Bordetella bronchiseptica*. It is often started by an injury to the snout. The symptoms are sneezing, tearing, and a runny nose. The nasal discharge is often foul-smelling. It is usually seen in pigs 3 to 8 weeks old. Veterinarian attention usually should be sought. It is treated with sulfonamides and/or antibiotics in feed and water.

Baby Pig Scours. This is a generalized term for a wide number of diarrhea-causing diseases in young pigs. See Colibacillosis, Enterotoxemia, Salmonellosis, and Coccidiosis.

Brucellosis. An infection caused by the bacteria, *Brucella suis*, it can also infect cattle and man. It is called undulant fever in humans. Symptons are usually seen in pregnant sows: abortion, weak piglets, stillborn piglets. It may cause sterility and hind paralysis or lame back legs. This requires prompt professional attention and disease confirmation. There is no treatment for brucellosis; you will have to slaughter infected animals when the diagnosis is confirmed. Contact your veterinarian for proper methods of disposal to prevent infection of other animals.

Cholera. Hog cholera is one of the most serious hog diseases and was responsible for many herd deaths in the past. Strict control measures and public awareness have lessened the problem today. No cases have been reported since 1976. Contact your veterinarian regarding the need to vaccinate in your area.

Cholera is a generalized disease caused by a virus which can survive in pickled and frozen pork products. Highly contagious, it affects swine of all ages and is characterized by high fever, gummy eyes, constipation, diarrhea, paralysis, convulsions, and death. Vaccination is available and is recommended in some parts of the country. Anti-serum can be used after exposure, but it isn't always successful in preventing the outbreak. All cases must be reported to the state veterinarian in most parts of the country. No other treatment is available except slaughter of the herd and proper disposal to avoid spreading the disease (contact your veterinarian).

Listless victims of hog cholera. (Photo courtesy USDA)

Coccidiosis. A form of enteritis or scours caused by the protozoa *Coccidia*, which causes inflammation of the small or large intestines. It is characterized by profuse, often bloody diarrhea and weight loss in pigs 1 to 3 months old. Most often, it is associated with damp, dirty pens. It is treated with sulfa drugs after a professional confirms the diagnosis.

Colibacillosis. Also known as enteric colibacillosis, enterotoxic colibacillosis, and *E. coli* scours, this is an infection of the small intestines caused by a virulent strain of the gut bacteria, *E. coli*. It it most often seen in young pigs and is characterized by weakness, chills, and blue skin coloring. Victims often die rapidly with or without diarrhea. Dehydration is common. It should be diagnosed by a professional before being treated with a number of antibacterial agents; resistant bacteria often develop.

Deficiency Diseases. A wide variety of symptoms are caused by dietary deficiencies. The most common are anemia, deficient protein, and starvation (deficient energy intake). Water deprivation can also cause disease symptoms. Treat by replacing the missing dietary element after a professional diagnosis.

Dysentery. Bloody diarrhea caused by the bacteria, *Treponema hyodysenteriae*, with symptoms that include rapid weight loss and dehydration. Treat with antibiotics after a professional diagnosis.

Enteritis. A term for a wide variety of diarrhea-characterized diseases. It is caused by infection or inflammation of the small or large intestines. A protein-deficient diet may be a cause. Symptoms include a lack of appetite, low energy level, diarrhea, and high temperature. This requires professional diagnosis. It is treated with antibiotics, if it is a bacterial infection. If caused by protein deficiency, the diet should be improved. *Necrotic enteritis* is the decay of the intestinal tissue resulting from an enteric disease that is either not treated or treated incorrectly.

Enterotoxemia. An infection caused by the bacteria *Clostridium perfringens*, resulting in severe diarrhea in very young pigs. Treat with antitoxin after a professional confirms the infection's cause.

Erysipelas. Several disease forms caused by a bacteria, *E. insi-diosa*, which is widespread in nature and persists in soil and water for very long periods. It causes an infectious disease in swine and a wound infection in humans. The disease ranges from inapparent to subacute, acute, and chronic. Stress seems to be a major factor in the disease development. Most often it is seen in pigs less than 3 weeks old. It is characterized by fever, lack of appetite, sore joints, weakness, and possible skin lesions in pink to purple diamond shapes. The chronic form appears as arthritis and heart-lining inflammation; survivors become carriers. A vaccination is available, but it is not always effective. It seems to be a local disease problem, so contact your veterinarian regarding the need to vaccinate. It is treated with penicillin if diagnosed early.

Hypoglycemia. This is the medical term for low blood sugar, a condition often affecting baby pigs whose mother has poor or no milk production. Death soon follows if nutrition is not improved. It can be treated by feeding piglets a dextrose solution with or without medical assistance.

Influenza. Swine influenza (not the same as the human "swine flu") is a highly contagious respiratory disease caused by a variety of adaptable viruses. Like the human flu, it is characterized by depression, fever, coughing, weakness, and a runny nose, and it most often appears in the fall and winter months. As with humans, it cannot be treated directly, but secondary infections are treated with antibiotics. If a professional diagnosis indicates that your hogs have influenza, treat by feeding only highest quality feed, offer plenty of clean water, and make sure that draft-free protection and ample bedding is available.

Leptospirosis. An infection of the kidneys by the *Leptospire* species of bacteria that is characterized by fever; dark, bloody urine; abortions; and weak newborn pigs. Treat with antibiotics after a professional diagnosis.

Lice. An external skin parasite. The small, grayish louse is visible to the naked eye. The infection is characterized by violent scratching, loss of appetite, and egg masses around the ears and neck. Lice can be treated without medical attention using an approved louse spray or powder (available at feed stores and animal hospitals). If your veterinarian recommends it for your area, your hogs can be periodically "dusted" to prevent lice outbreaks.

Mange. This is the most extensive external skin parasite in swine. Infestation is characterized by intense itching and weight loss. The tiny invisible mites burrow into the skin and cannot be seen with the naked eye. The pig's constant scratching may cause the skin to be literally rubbed raw unless the condition is professionally diagnosed and treated. Sprays and powders are available to prevent and treat mange. Some are effective against both lice and mange. Contact your local veterinarian for prevention advice.

Myiasis. Invasion of animal tissue by a fly larvae. The screwworm has the only fly maggot that regularly eats living flesh after the adult fly lays her eggs in open wounds. Prevent by taking immediate care of any open sores, calling in professional assistance when needed. Treat by having the infected wound professionally cleaned and disinfected.

Mycoplasma Pneumonia. An infection of the respiratory organs caused by the *Mycoplasma* virus. Not like other pneumonias in that there is no fever or lack of appetite, but it is characterized by continuous coughing. Treat with sulfonamides after a professional diagnosis.

Pasteurellosis. Also called "shipping fever." Usually a complication of pneumonia, this is a lung disease caused by the *Pasteurella* species of bacteria. Symptoms include high fever and sudden death. Immediate attention by a veterinarian is needed. Treat by early use of anitbiotics.

Pneumonia. Inflammation of the respiratory tract that may be caused by bacteria, viruses, inhaled dust, or a number of other factors. Often a secondary infection following influenza or a period of high stress. Animals infected go off feed, breathe hard (wheeze), have a high fever, and are weak. They need to be seen by a doctor immediately because rapid death is not uncommon. Treat with antibiotics after a professional diagnosis.

Pseudorabies. A highly contagious viral infection of the brains and nerves, most common in pigs less than 3 months old. Pigs may develop paralysis, go into a coma, and die within 24 hours. Although no treatment is currently available except isolation of infected animals, professional help should be called.

PSS. Porcine Stress Syndrome (PSS) seems to be a genetic condition that causes death at shipping or other times of high stress. It is particularly noticeable in confinement conditions. No treatment is available, but professional advice should be sought.

Rickets. A bone and joint disorder caused by several dietary deficiencies including vitamin D, calcium, and phosphorus. Once the deficiency has been confirmed by a professional diagnosis, replace the missing nutrient in the animal's diet.

Salmonellosis. Also known as *paratyphoid*, this is an infection of the intestines caused by *Salmonella* bacteria. This organism is also responsible for a human form of food poisoning. Rodents are often carriers, and the disease is frequently contracted from contaminated feed, water, or bedding. The bacteria multiplies rapidly in moist feed and liquids. Because the organism is widespread in nature, the disease depends on the dose, the animal's resistance and stress level, as well as the particular organism involved. The disease forms resemble so many other illnesses that diagnosis is often difficult.

The subacute form of the disease is characterized by frequent, often bloody diarrhea, red and purple skin discolorations, a high fever, blood poisoning, and rapid death, often within 24 hours. The subacute form most often strikes pigs less than 4 months old. The acute disease takes the same form as human food poisoning: fever, cramps, watery diarrhea, lack of appetite, extreme thirst, and dehydration. The chronic form results in persistent diarrhea with the bacteria shed in the feces from the bile ducts and gall bladder.

Professional diagnosis and advice is crucial with this disease. Treatment of all forms is with antibiotics and fluids.

Transmissible Gastroenteritis [TGE]. A highly contagious viral disease with high mortality rates especially among young animals, TGE is characterized by diarrhea, vomiting, severe dehydration, and weight loss. Vaccinations are available; ask your local veterinarian if they are needed in your area. If you suspect TGE, call for a professional diagnosis immediately as rapid death is common. Antibiotics often help.

Trichinosis. A parasitic disease of swine and humans caused by the microscopic nematode worm, *Trichinella spiralis*, which burrows into the animal's flesh. It is usually caused in humans by eating infested raw or undercooked pork and wild game. It is most prevalent where uncooked garbage (containing the worms) is fed to swine, especially if rats, which can be infected and eaten by swine as well, are also present. After being consumed, the adult parasite produces numerous young in the host animal's intestines. The larvae migrate through the intestinal wall, into the bloodstream, and finally into the animal's muscles. Here, they grow to 1/25 inch long, roll into a spiral shape and surround themselves with a capsule. They may live in this stage for years.

Trichinosis is difficult to diagnose in swine as it produces no symptoms except an occasional low-grade fever that may be confused with many other minor diseases. In humans, the disease symptoms vary according to the degree of infestation. It is usually accompanied by fever, muscle swelling and pain, and digestive disturbances which begin about 2 weeks after eating the infected meat. Diagnosis in humans is made with a skin test.

Although this disease is nearly eradicated, prevention is still a prime concern of all pork producers. Begin by eliminating all rats on the farm. Then, cook all garbage at 212 degrees F. for at least 30 minutes before feeding it to your hogs. Finally, cook all pork products thoroughly before consuming.

If you are concerned about the possibility of trichinosis in your area, call on your local veterinarian for advice.

Worms. Pigs are subject to inhabitation by several species of parasitic worms besides the one that causes trichinosis. In fact, it is the biggest health problem most raisers are likely to face, and some experts say that it is nearly impossible to have a 100 percent worm-free herd. The most common swine parasites are stomach, heart, intestinal, and lung worms. Low-level infestations have minimal effects, but high levels can cause retarded growth, a pot belly, and diarrhea. Commercial dewormers (anthelmintics) are valuable to control worm populations in areas where worm infestation is a real problem and in large animal herds. We don't recommend that you routinely worm your hogs, however, unless a professional diagnosis so indicates. Misuse of anthelmintics can cause more harm than the worms. If you are concerned about worms in your animals, have a veterinarian diagnose the presence of worm species from a stool sample and prescribe specific dewormers for your hogs. Anthelmintics usually are mixed into feed or water.

We have not covered every disease a pig can possibly get. In fact, we see no reason to go into more detail about pig ailments. We don't want to scare you away from raising pigs, after all. If you raise only a couple of pigs at a time (like we do) and only during the mild months of the year (like we do), then you probably will never have to worry about disease (we haven't). Nonetheless, if you have a question, the best place to find the answer is at your local veterinarian's office. Lacking that, we recommend that you talk to someone who has been raising pigs in your area for many years, or you might try reading one of the excellent veterinarian's manuals listed in Appendix C.

Chapter 8

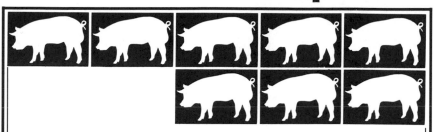

USING
WHAT'S LEFT:
MANURE MANAGEMENT

Let's face it: pigs produce their fair share of waste, and you will need to do something with it. During the finishing period (from 30 pounds to market weight of 200 to 220 pounds), an average hog will leave behind 4,600 pounds of manure. That's more than 1.5 tons of waste per 100 pounds live weight per year. To put it yet another way, a 100-pound hog will produce ⅛ cubic foot, 1 gallon, or 7.5 pounds of manure per day. A market-weight hog will produce more than double that. If you want or need even more explicit figures, Table 8–1 will give them to you. On farms where several hundred or thousand head of swine are raised annually, this amounts to a massive amount of waste that must be handled.

Generally speaking, the term "manure" refers to a mixture of animal excrement (undigested feed and body wastes) and any bedding material that may be mixed in during removal. Most livestock writers don't like to deal much with manure—and neither do many farmers. To be honest, it is a very smelly subject and nobody can honestly say that they enjoy it. However, this animal end-product can be a valuable resource or an unwanted irritant depending on how you view it and how you use it.

MANURE REMOVAL

Most large-scale operations deal with the problem in as quick and easy a way as possible. Confinement-reared hogs, are generally raised on slotted floors which allow manure and urine to drop into a pit below the pens. Manure is either allowed to collect in the pits below the buildings or it is liquified and piped to a lagoon or holding tank. A lagoon is a body of water or a pond into which liquified manure is discharged and digested by bacterial action. Although much of the fertilizer value is wasted, this method gets the manure off the floor or out of the holding pits as quickly and efficiently as possible. Most confinement systems usually include some sort of

Table 8-1

MANURE PRODUCTION

Nursery Pig (35 lbs.)	2.3 lbs./day	.038 cu.ft./day	0.27 gal./day
Growing Pig (65 lbs.)	4.2	.070	0.48
Finishing Pig (150 lbs.)	9.8	.160	1.13
Market Hog (200 lbs.)	13.0	.022	1.50

(From: Washington State University Cooperative Extensive Service, Pork Industry Handbook #EM4165, September 1979.)

Table 8–1. *Manure is 91% water; these figures are for urine and feces only, no bedding or dilution water.*

mechanical ventilation to remove the odors and gases. In these large-scale cases, the liquified waste is used eventually on fields destined for crops via an irrigation system.

Large quantities of unattended manure not only cause offensive odors around confinement swine buildings, but they may be an indirect source of disease. Therefore, proper and regular removal is essential for large and small operations when hogs are housed in limited pen space. Once a week cleaning of confinement facilities should be considered a minimum requirement for your pigs' and your own health and well-being.

Other manure disposal techniques vary according to the type of living conditions your hogs have.

When only a few hogs are housed in a small to medium-size pen, they will establish a "bathroom corner." Depending on the number of pigs and the size of the pen, removal should be scheduled every week or two. If the hogs suddenly start using another corner for their waste or if they begin relieving themselves near their bed area, that's a good indication that the manure needs to be removed.

Manure removal from a small pen usually is accomplished with a pitchfork and a shovel. We toss the waste over the fence and into a large wheelbarrow on the other side. Some farmers bring the wheelbarrow into the pen with them, but we've found that getting the cart out the gate without releasing the animals tends to be a bit tricky. Needless to say, hogs get very curious about what you are doing in their bathroom, especially if you bring along some unfamiliar toy like a wheelbarrow.

If your hogs are penned on a concrete floor, hose the area down after removing the manure. If, on the other hand, the pen has a dirt floor like ours, spread a 2-inch to 4-inch layer of sawdust or even "kitty litter" in the bathroom corner after cleaning to absorb odors and excess moisture. In fact, sawdust can be used an inch or two at a time in that area to absorb urine and control flies between cleanings.

Pastured and land-clearing hogs usually automatically distribute their manure over the land. It generally does not need to be removed and your chores will be minimized. The manure can be left where it was deposited to decay and fertilize the soil if you rotate the hogs to another area before the field gets muddy.

Occasionally, however, pigs on pasture or in land-clearing lots will, like their penned relatives, establish a "bathroom area" and use it exclusively. The manure must then be removed from the bathroom corner every few weeks. Sawdust can be spread in the area to help absorb excess urine and control the odors and flies.

WHAT TO DO WITH THE MANURE

Except in the case of only 2 to 6 hogs, environmental controls regulate how and where manure can be disposed. Direct run-off into surface or ground water is controlled by federal and/or state laws. State and local agencies often limit how and when waste can be applied to the land. Finally, state laws regulate the amount of "air pollution" (odors) allowed. When in doubt, a visit to the local extension agent may be in order.

Other than give it away, you basically have 2 options when it comes to hog manure: fertilizer and fuel.

Back to the Land With That Manure

Swine waste is an excellent organic fertilizer and soil additive. Ninety percent of the potassium and eighty percent of the nitrogen and phosphorus in the pig ration is excreted again by the animal in a chemically simpler form. It compares favorably to manures of other farm animals for fertilizing merit. Further, when added to the soil it prevents soil crusting, improves soil structure, and provides food for beneficial soil organisms, such as earthworms.

Hog manure varies in fertilizing value according to the animal's diet and age, among other factors. Excrement from young, growing pigs is not as rich in nutrients as that of mature animals.

The fertilizing usefulness is best and the nutrient losses are minimized if the manure is applied to the land as soon as possible and then mixed by digging or plowing immediately into the soil. When spread directly on gardens or fields in this manner, 25 pounds of manure is enough to enrich and condition 100 square feet of land area. It should be applied at least 4 weeks before planting.

A very thin layer of green (fresh) manure can be spread on pastures and lawns without plowing under to benefit their growth. Don't get carried away, however, or the plants could smother. Water the manure into the ground thoroughly or wait to apply until just before a heavy rain is expected.

Some crops, such as corn and leafy plants, respond favorably to green or aged manure in the soil. Others, like the cereal grains and root crops, may grow large, luxurious plants, but at the expense of the grain or the roots. Also, fields that have been manured before planting are best for grasses that have high nitrogen requirements, rather than legumes that fix nitrogen from the air via root bacteria. When in doubt about which fields or garden spaces would benefit the most from your swine manure, consult an extension agricultural agent or a good gardening manual.

Fresh swine waste, like most other livestock manures, is "hot"— that is, it will burn tender seedlings and young roots if applied directly to most crops. Hence, many farmers age or compost manure with other animal and vegetable materials before applying to land where crops are already growing.

Pretreating or aging raw manure prior to land application is done to reduce the biological strength, the nutrient concentration, and/or the odor-producing potential. It is almost impossible to entirely prevent nutrient losses during aging or storage. To reduce these losses, however, locate the manure heap on a level or slightly dished area to minimize leaching and run-off. Cover with a thin layer of topsoil if the pile will sit for a long time before it is used.

A ton of well-preserved hog manure, free of bedding, contains plant-food nutrients equal to about 100 pounds of commercial 10-2-7 fertilizer and should be spread at the rate of 8 tons per acre.

Manure Tea

A weak liquid prepared by seeping fresh manure in water is very useful for houseplants, to give flower plants a boost before they start to bloom, and to establish transplants. The following recipe is very easy and will make enough tea for an entire growing season.

Fill a 100-pound burlap sack with fresh manure. Suspend the bag in a 60-gallon steel drum and fill the container with warm water. Cover the drum and let the manure seep for 30 to 40 days at a moderate to warm temperature (55 to 85 degrees F.). Remove the bag and add water to fill the drum to within 1 inch of the top.

Manure tea is best if applied liberally and washed into the soil with water or before a good rain. One gallon per 5 square feet of plant bed is sufficient for most flowers, vegetables, and shrubs.

How to Make Compost

Another way to use swine manure is to make a compost heap with other waste materials, such as bedding hay, leaves, and grass clippings. Composting is a way of returning a great amount of *humus* (the dark, gummy, clean-smelling substance derived from animal and plant breakdown products) back to the soil.

To make a compost heap, sandwich vegetable layers (leaves, lawn clippings, hay, sawdust, even wet newspapers) between layers of nitrogen-rich substances, such as manure and topsoil. With adequate air and water, the waste materials will be transformed by bacterial action into humus in a matter of about 3 months in the summer. The high heat (up to 150 degrees F.) of composting rapidly "cooks" the stink out of manure. Further, much of the carbon is "burned off" by the bacteria, and this increases the proportion of nitrogen in the pile, making compost an excellent fertilizer and soil additive.

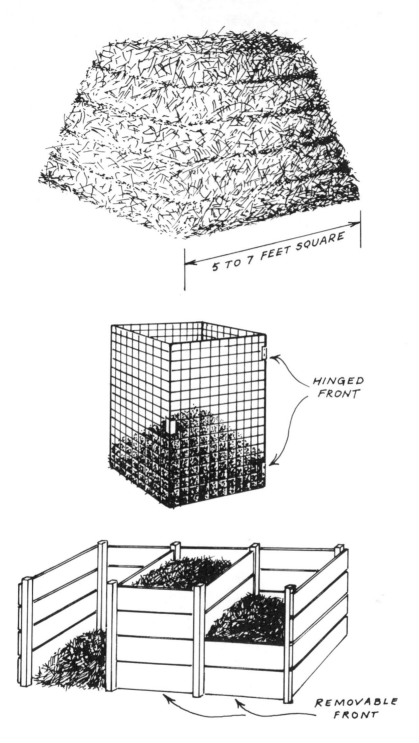

5 TO 7 FEET SQUARE

HINGED
FRONT

REMOVABLE
FRONT

Some suggested composting methods

Locate your compost pile on a flat or slightly concave piece of ground close enough to your supply of manure and other wastes to eliminate lengthy hauls. You can form the heap either with or without sidewalls. Avoid solid sides, however, because air circulation is essential to the bacterial action.

Start with a 1 foot layer of vegetable matter. Water it well. Add an inch of manure and cover with 2 inches of soil (urine-soaked soil is the most valuable). Wood ashes can then be sprinkled on the top of the dirt layer, if desired, to add even more minerals to the finished product.

Continue this layering until the pile is 5 to 7 feet high. Avoid woody materials (which take a long time to break down), cooked or greasy food scraps, and weed seeds. Cover the finished pile with a 6-inch layer of soil, slightly caved in at the center to catch the rainwater.

Keep the pile moist, but not soggy. Water every 2 weeks during a dry summer. Cover the heap with plastic during very wet weather. If the pile gets too wet, the microorganisms will smother and composting will stop.

Some gardeners turn the pile every couple of weeks with a pitchfork to guarantee that all areas are exposed to air and bacterial decay. Supposedly, this hastens the composting. We never turn our piles, however. We'd rather wait the extra few weeks for finished compost than hassle with turning the heap.

When the compost is finished, the temperature of the pile will go back to normal and what you'll have is black or dark-brown, sweet-smelling "super-soil." Dig 1 to 3 inches of compost into the top 4 inches of soil a month or two before planting. Compost can be added in this manner once or twice a year. It can also be spread thinly on lawns or mulched thickly around trees and shrubs.

Another way to produce a compost of sorts also produces another valuable resource: earthworms. A compost mixture of 70 percent vegetable matter, 15 percent manure, and 12 percent soil makes an excellent growth medium for wormbeds.

Mix the raw materials together and fill boxes that are 2 to 3 feet square and about 2 feet high. You can "seed" the boxes with purchased worms, or wait for those already in your soil to move in (we guarantee they will come). Just keep the beds moist, not drenched, and within 60 days the wigglers will have turned all that waste into valuable worm casings. Plus, they will have reproduced several times over.

When the worms have finished their work, remove half the composted material and replace it with fresh raw waste. Use the compost on your garden and then go fishing with the worms!

Biogas From Swine Manure

Swine manure, like most animal waste, has the potential to be used to produce energy. The process happens all the time in nature all by itself: In the absence of oxygen, bacteria convert the manure and urine into a burnable methane gas very similar to the natural gas used to heat homes and cook food. It's called *biogas*, and it can be burned for heat and used to power engines which generate electricity.

Biogas production, although not difficult, does require a high initial investment in equipment, much daily labor, and careful operation for safety and optimum usable gas. Further, some experts have estimated that you need the manure from 200 hogs being raised for pork to heat a well-insulated, 3-bedroom home.

Considering the equipment required, the labor demands, and the need for a very large, continuous hog operation, this is not something that would be feasible or profitable for the raiser of a couple of pork animals. Thus, for the small hog operation, we suggest that you use the waste that your hogs produce to fertilize your gardens or those of your friends and neighbors.

Chapter 9

FROM
PIG TO PORK:
BUTCHERING

When your hogs are 5 to 6 months old and weigh 220 to 230 pounds, the time has come to think about butchering. Additional feeding beyond this point will produce fat and the rate of gain will be less. The biggest questions you will probably consider at this point are:

- **How much pork can I expect to get from a 220-pound live hog?**
- **How can I tell if my pork-raising venture has been profitable? Am I really paying less per pound by raising it myself?**
- **Should I send my porkers out to the local slaughterhouse or butcher them myself?**

CALCULATING PORK RETURNS

On the average, a hog will dress out at 65 to 75 percent of its live weight. (For comparison, a beef cow dresses out at 60 percent and a lamb at 50 percent.) That is, a 220-pound hog will produce a 154-pound to 175-pound carcass which will be 17 to 22 percent legs (hams), 11 to 17 percent side (bacon, spareribs), 11 to 16 percent loins (roasts, chops), 17 to 19 percent shoulders (roasts), 9 percent head, 19 to 20 percent fat, plus some miscellaneous cuts— hocks, jowl, and neckbones. If you plan to use the specialty meats (liver, heart, brains, kidneys, etc.) and lard, your final pork return will be even greater than the 120 pounds of retail cuts normally expected from a 220-pound hog.

GRADING BUTCHER HOGS

Commercially, the modern meat hog is graded and valued before slaughtering. This grading is determined by the amount of backfat and the loin eye area, which is the band of muscle running parallel to the backbone. Grading is not necessary for the small-scale pork producer unless you sell quite a bit of your pork on the commercial market (which we assume you won't). Also large-scale producers use expensive ultrasound equipment to determine the backfat and loin eye measurements when several hundred head need to be measured before being sent to the slaughterhouse. Purchase of this equipment is very expensive and not recommended for the small-scale raiser.

The old-fashioned way to measure backfat thickness on a live animal (before the availability of ultrasound) is a simple knife-and-ruler technique still used by some producers. We have never tried this and we don't recommend that you try it either unless experienced assistance is available. We feel the backfat and loin eye measurements received after the animal is slaughtered are sufficient for our information, and we have never been curious enough to probe into a live animal's fat layer with a knife.

CALCULATING COST PER POUND

The biggest question most small-scale pork raisers ask is how much does it really cost for that pork, per pound. Are you really paying less than supermarket prices by raising it yourself?

To figure your cost per pound, first calculate a base cost per hog that includes the price you paid for the weaner pig, feed and supplements, veterinary expenses, and housing and equipment. To be fair, housing and equipment costs should be spread out (amortized) over the number of years it will be used. We will assume that most housing and hog equipment will last 5 years, so divide that total cost by 5 before adding it to the cost of the pig, its total feed bill, and any medical expenses.

To the base cost, add any slaughter or butchering expenses. This figure is your total hog-raising cost (we're ignoring your labor) which you divide by the number of usable pounds of pork you got after butchering to figure cost per pound.

We have prepared Table 9–1 based on our costs to raise 2 pigs from weaner to butcher size (about 6 months) in 1983.

Your costs will not be the same as ours because weaner pig and feed costs vary in different areas of the country and at different times of the year. Also, if you feed a homegrown diet (we feed a commercial ration for the most part), your costs will be considerably less. But, if you use all new building materials for your pig housing, your raising costs will go up. The amount of medical attention you hogs require will also affect your final calculations. Finally, slaughter and butcher expenses fluctuate substantially.

Take your final calculation to your local grocery store or butcher shop and compare: do you feel it was worth it? Sure, some retail pork cuts will cost more than your final price-per-pound figure and some will cost far less, but you are concerned mainly with the average and with the going rate for pork sides. Also keep in mind that you know what your hog ate, so your homegrown pork doesn't contain many of the questionable additives fed to commercial hogs. Additionally, if your hogs cleared out a section of undeveloped land while they were growing up, you can also figure in the bulldozing expenses you saved.

SEND OUT OR BUTCHER AT HOME?

Give careful consideration to several factors before you decide who will butcher Porky. First of all, think about the expense. Unless you plan to sell part of the pork to defray the costs, having your pork prepared at a commercial slaughterhouse is not cheap. Furthermore, if there isn't a packing plant nearby, transporting costs (and these can be substantial) must also be considered. Then, there is the stress associated with moving the hog from a home he knows and trusts to strange surroundings that may frighten him and could conceivably change the meat quality.

On the other hand, consider that slaughtering and butchering your hog yourself is a difficult chore (actually, it's 2 distinct jobs) that may take several days if you're a novice—and you probably won't end up with the nice, even cuts of meat that you see in the butcher's

Table 9-1

COSTS OF A TWO-PIG OPERATION

Cost of 2 weaner pigs at $35.00 each	$ 70.00
Housing and fencing:	
• Recycled & scrap lumber used extensively	
• $50.00 total cost divided by 5 years	10.00
Feed: 600 pounds of commercial ration, purchased bulk, per pig at $.10 per pound	120.00
Veterinary expenses, two pigs	NONE
BASE COST, 2 pigs from weaner to butcher	$200.00
Outside slaughter and butcher expenses:	
• Hauling, 2 pigs at $6.00 each	12.00
• Slaughter, 2 pigs at $17.00 each	34.00
• Cut & wrap meat at $.17 per pound	
* 150 lbs. meat per pig	
* 150 × $.17 = $25.50 per pig	51.00
• Smoking bacon & hams at $.25 per pound	
* 40 pounds smoked meat per pig	
* 40 × $.25 = $10.00 per pig	20.00
• Slicing bacon at $2.00 per pig	4.00
• Sales tax on slaughter/butcher services	9.00
TOTAL OUTSIDE BUTCHERING EXPENSE, 2 pigs	$130.00
BASE COST, 2 pigs (above)	200.00
TOTAL COST of producing 2 pigs' worth of pork	$330.00
• Each pig produced 150 pounds usable/salable meat	
* 150 × 2 = 300 pounds pork	
* $330.00 total cost divided by 300 pounds pork gives us a cost-per-pound of $1.10	

Table 9-1.   *These figures represent our costs to raise 2 pigs in 1983. The average pork cost in our area at this time was $1.25 to $1.39 per pound.*

display case. After all, a professional can whiz through cuts, bone and all, with a powerful electric band saw. Home butchering requires tedious back and forth sawing by hand.

We usually send our hogs out to be slaughtered simply because we don't want the work of preparing the meat ourselves and because, emotionally, we tend to grow attached to the porkers. It is far easier to pat them good-bye as they leave in the truck and welcome them back in white paper wrappers. The act of killing something you have raised from a baby is not an easy task, no matter what experienced farm-butchers might tell you!

Another point in favor of sending the hogs out to a commercial packing plant is the USDA stamp on the carcass that assures us that our animals have passed the standard on-the-hoof and carcass inspections and they were carrying no diseases at the time of slaughter. Although we assume that our hogs are healthy, diseases can be overlooked easily during home butcher. That USDA stamp of approval eases many subtle doubts. Furthermore, all meat that is to be sold or traded for human consumption must be slaughtered in an approved facility under the supervision of a state or USDA meat inspector.

CUSTOM BUTCHERING

We are lucky because there is a reliable butcher nearby who we have come to trust over many years of doing business. If you are thinking about selecting a slaughterhouse and/or butchering facility for the first time, shop around before making a final choice. You can locate slaughterhouses and custom butchers in the telephone yellow pages under the listings "Meat—Wholesale" and "Meat—Retail." You might also get some leads by talking to other pork raisers, feed stores, and your county cooperative extension agent.

Visit each plant in your area. Does it look and smell clean? Talk to the owner and ask about prices. Not only do slaughterhouses vary widely in rates charged, they also differ in the quality of workmanship, the amount of time a hog is held before killing, and the length of time it takes to get the meat processed and back to you. Ideally, your animals should be killed and slaughtered the same day they are hauled to the plant (certainly they should be held alive no longer than 24 hours). Then, the best custom butchers will have your meat cut, wrapped, frozen, and ready to be picked up in 3 days or less.

Another factor to keep in mind is that some butchers assume that they keep much of the specialty meats, backfat, hide, and even the head unless you specifically ask for them. Try to locate an establishment that routinely gives you back everything from the carcass and lets you decide what to consider edible and what is waste. However, be aware that most processors keep the hide if an animal is skinned (butcher hogs under 300 pounds are normally scalded and scraped with the hide left intact in commercial slaughter-houses).

The basic agreement between a farmer and a butcher is that the client receives all of the meat cut up as directed. Be prepared for questions about thickness of steaks and chops, number of pounds per package, and size of roasts. Get everything settled before bringing your hog to the plant.

Contrary to popular beliefs, animal switching at the slaughter-house is rare because each animal is tattooed when it enters the plant. Then, each side of pork is matched and marked during or after slaughter. Also, carcass and meat switching and stealing during the cutting stage probably is claimed more often than it actually happens. Nonetheless, for your own peace of mind, find a butcher-ing operation that allows you to witness the cutting and wrapping procedures if you so desire. Be wary of any meat cutter who won't allow you to watch.

Transporting your hog from pen to *abattoir* (slaughterhouse) will be the next problem you must solve once you have chosen a butcher you can trust. Basically, you can transport your hogs your-self (if you have a large, sturdy truck) or you can pay to have it done (transport by others costs about $1 per mile in 1983 in our area). In either case, you'll need a ramp to the truck from the pen (we hope that you located your pigpen so that a truck can get relatively close to it) — preferably one with the sideways vision restricted by boards, gates, or panels. Hogs are not always cooperative about being loaded, so plan to have several helpers around on transport day. Then, follow the suggestions given in chapter 7 for moving hogs.

Routinely, all feed (but not water) is withheld from an animal for 24 hours before butcher. Withholding feed is usually done for the sake of the butcher (less mess when the intestines and stomach are empty) and to save wasted feed. Some raisers don't do it because they say that it upsets the animal to miss feedings and adds to the stress level on butchering day.

We've found that withholding feed can be helpful when you plan to transport. A hungry hog often can be enticed into a truck bed with a little corn rattling in a bucket. Just make sure that his at-tention is not diverted from the goal by an interesting view across the pasture. If the ramp itself does not have side walls, have several helpers limit the animal's vision and outside access with gates and solid panels. As with recapturing an escaped hog, moving one requires quiet determination—loud yelling or chasing only frightens the animal and defeats your purpose.

"Shrink loss," the amount of weight hogs lose during transit to market, is a function of distance and time. Most hogs, no matter how close to the slaughterhouse, will shrink about 2 to 4 percent simply from the stress of riding in the truck and the new surroundings. If the shipping is over 150 miles or the transit handling is particularly rough and stressful, especially in hot weather, losses can exceed 8 percent. Further, the stress of moving and being held too long in the slaughterhouse before killing (holding a live animal longer than 24 hours is too long) can cause PSW (pale, soft, watery) pork. A rapid, abnormally large buildup of lactic acid in the muscle fibers produces a lighter colored, two-tone, watery form of pork with poor eating qualities. The enzyme that normally breaks the acid down isn't functioning. Although stress is definitely the cause, it is not known exactly how the condition occurs. PSW pork is most often associated with crowded commercial transit and slaughterhouse conditions, but it pays to be careful even with only a few hogs: make the transport as short and comfortable as possible and make sure that slaughter occurs very soon after arrival at the facility.

Some pork raisers prefer to have their animals killed on the farm to avoid the stress of moving. Bleeding out and gutting are also performed in the pen or an area nearby and then the carcass, usually cut into halves, is transported to the butcher or kept on the farm for cutting and wrapping.

The farm-kill slaughter method may be worth the added expense for the first-timer because watching a professional in action is a true education. In 1984, a hog could be farm-killed by a professional at a cost of $15 to $20 in our area, and farm-slaughtered meat is ready for chilling and cutting and wrapping in less than an hour. Keep in mind, however, that unless a meat inspector is on hand for the event, the pork cannot be sold or traded for human consumption. In fact, in many states, only approved facilities can produce meat for retail sale or trade.

HOME BUTCHER

You've considered the alternatives and you still want to butcher your hog yourself—perhaps for financial reasons, perhaps simply because you want to see if you can do it, perhaps for the satisfaction of knowing exactly where the meat on your table came from. Why not? Although no longer a common practice, Grandpa butchered his own animals, so can you. Just remember that you cannot sell or trade the meat. It must be used only by your household. Also, if it is your first time, enlist the aid of an experienced friend or neighbor with the proper tools (you'll need help to hoist a dead 220-pound hog around anyway). Hands-on assistance is far better than trying to follow the directions in this or any other book.

One of the best, easiest-to-follow home butchering guides we have seen is a well-illustrated gem from USDA (Farmers' Bulletin Number 2265, *Pork: Slaughtering, Cutting, Preserving, and Cooking on the Farm*). Because this booklet is so well done and because we have never attempted home butcher, most of the following home-butcher directions are from this USDA publication.

It almost goes without saying that you should not select an unhealthy animal for slaughter. If you have questions at all, plan to have a veterinarian out to examine the hog before you butcher.

To obtain the highest quality meat, exercise proper care of the animal prior to slaughter. Most experts recommend that you restrict feed for 24 hours, but maintain access to clean water. Withholding food minimizes the feces released after death and an empty bowel is less likely to be punctured during slaughter.

Some farmers clean their animals with soap and water prior to butcher. This isn't necessary unless the animal is very dirty. If you plan to scald and scrape the skin, the dirt will be removed then. If you would rather skin the hog and tan the pigskin, the outer layer of skin (with the hair and any dirt) will be removed before tanning.

Keep the animal calm and quiet. Do not chase or otherwise excite hogs on butcher day as the stress will increase the risks of stress-related meat problems.

Slaughter Site and Equipment

Well before the slaughter day, select the site and accumulate the needed equipment. If this is a one-time venture, it is best to borrow rather than buy necessary tools, as the cost of the necessary tools may be substantial.

Select a site where a fire can be built (if you are scalding instead of skinning), with access to clean, running water. You'll also need a sturdy tree limb or block-and-tackle from which to suspend the carcass. If the butchering will take place indoors, a strong beam will work.

Clean the site carefully, disinfecting concrete or wooden floors with plenty of soap and water. Rinse thoroughly. If you are using an outdoor site, cover the slaughter area with fresh straw.

Have a garbage can ready for butchering waste and make sure that blood and water can drain away from the carcass without polluting nearby streams or other water supplies. Arrange to have a local processor or rendering plant pick up the butchering waste if possible. If you plan to bury the viscera and hair, they must be planted deeply so that dogs and other animals cannot dig them up. Hair can be burned.

As a minimum, you will need the following equipment: a .22 caliber rifle or other weapon to kill the animal; a sharp skinning knife and steel; a boning knife; a block-and-tackle or chain hoist strong enough to hold the weight of the slaughtered animal; and meat saws (cleavers tend to chip the bone).

If you are scraping the animal rather than skinning it, you will also need one or two 50-gallon drums or other containers large enough to hold the hog and the boiling water, as well as a thermometer for the water and bell scrapers to remove the outer hair. Additional equipment will be needed for sectioning the carcass into pork cuts.

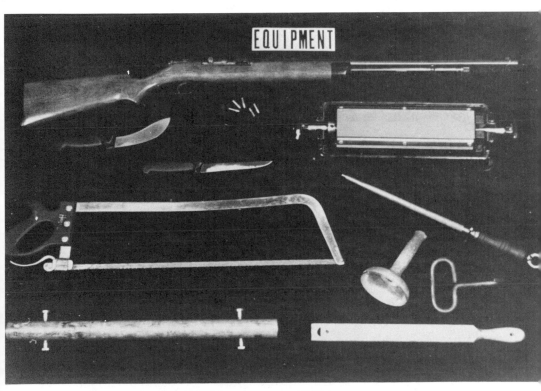

Equipment for slaughter (Photo courtesy USDA)

Time of the year is an important factor to consider when planning to butcher. Fall is normally chosen because the fly and yellow jacket populations have been killed back by early frosts and the nights are cool enough to chill a carcass without refrigeration. However, spring is an excellent choice as well and for the same reasons. During warm weather, plan to slaughter in the cool morning or evening hours to avoid exposing the carcass to high temperatures for long periods of time, which would increase the risk of spoilage. Also avoid extremely cold weather as freezing the carcass before it is permitted to chill naturally will result in less tender meat.

Much folklore surrounds animal butcher. Some old-timers never slaughter during a full moon because they believe that the animal won't bleed out properly. Others claim proper bleeding only occurs when a crescent moon has its tips up—or down. Some folk practices have their roots in common sense, but others (including moon shape) probably won't affect the quality of the butchering you do as much as the time and effort you put into the job.

Although a professional can slaughter a hog and have it ready for chilling in less than an hour, novices should expect to spend at least 3 to 4 hours per pig in the slaughter stage.

Killing and Bleeding

Killing the animal is perhaps the most difficult part of the entire butchering process. To say the least, it should be accomplished quickly and as humanely as possible.

Some so-called experts say to merely cut the jugular vein, without stunning or shooting, and simply allow the animal to bleed to death. Supposedly, this is painless. We have our doubts!

The most common method on farms is to shoot the animal with a .22 rifle in the forehead midway between and slightly above the eyes. If you are not an expert marksman, leave this chore to an experienced gun handler. Improperly placed bullets could cause the animal much pain or injure workers and other livestock. Further, animals who are excited by wounding will not bleed out as completely. Whenever using firearms, always exercise appropriate precautions!

Most slaughter plants immobilize hogs with electrical stunning or suffocation with carbon dioxide gas. Some farms also use mechanical stunners (or even a heavy hammer) to strike a sharp blow to the animal's forehead.

The hog should be bled within 2 minutes after it is down to avoid any discoloring in the meat from ruptured capillaries. Place the animal on its back, perfectly straight with the head close to the ground. Locate the tip of the breast bone, along the midline, and thrust a 6-inch sticking knife or skinning knife under the breastbone with the point aimed toward the tail. Give a quick, firm upward thrust to sever the cartoid artery. Twisting or cross-cutting is not usually needed. Take care not to stick the knife tip into the shoulder meat.

Most experts recommend leaving the animal on its back until the bleeding stops. Some farmers may want to save the blood for sausage or other reasons and will hang the animal by its hind legs for the bleeding, catching the liquid in a clean container.

Hair or Skin Removal

After bleeding is complete, the hair is removed by scalding in hot water and scraping, or the skin and hair can be removed by skinning. Traditionally, butcher-weight and smaller hogs are scalded and scraped and the skin is left intact. Although skinning is usually considered easier and faster and it requires less equipment, skinned hams don't keep as well as hams with a skin covering. Further, a bad skinning job that cuts into the meat can lower the pork quality significantly. However, if you skin the animal, you have a pigskin with which to practice your tanning skills.

Skinning

Skinning a hog is difficult because of the thick, undefined fat layer. There is no clear separation between skin and fat and the procedure tends to resemble skinning a watermelon. However, the method is similar to that used for beef, sheep, deer, and other large-animal carcasses.

Some skill is required to avoid damaging the meat, especially the bacon, so if you are inclined to skin, but have never attempted it before, follow a good instruction manual or, better yet, get experienced help.

The initial skinning steps are carried out while the animal is still on its back on a concrete or wooden slab after bleeding is complete. If you hoisted the animal up to save the blood, lower it back to the ground before beginning the skinning operation. The carcass can be held in place on its back by tucking concrete blocks under each side.

Using a sharp skinning knife, cut the hide around the rear legs, just below the dew claws. Be careful; you only want to cut the skin, not the meat. Then make a cut down the backs (toward the tail) of the rear legs, over the hocks, and to the midline (middle of the stomach) at the center of the hams. Skin around each side of the leg, removing the hide to a point below the hock. Use your fingers between the skin and the carcass as much as possible, using the tip of the skinning knife to loosen areas that stick.

After the rear legs are skinned, open the hide down the midline of the stomach from the jowls to the anus. Avoid the pubis area. Also, avoid cutting too deeply as you could puncture the intestines and contaminate the meat. Make this cut by inserting the point of the skinning knife under the skin with the blade turned up and away from the meat (this is called cutting from the inside out and protects the meat from contamination and accidental slices).

Cut from the stomach midline to the center of the inside of the hams. Be very careful as it is very easy to cut through the fat at this point and damage the carcass. To remove the skin, use a pulling-slicing technique: grasp the loosened hide in one hand and hold the knife in the other. Pull the hide up and out. This places tension on the hide, removes wrinkles, and allows the knife to glide smoothly. Always keep the knife blade turned slightly outward, away from the meat.

Skin the hams completely and continue along the sides toward the breast. Skin as far down the sides, from the stomach toward the backbone, as possible. This is called "siding."

When you have skinned as much as possible with the pig in the prone position, expose the gambrel tendons by cutting through the skin on the backs of the rear legs from the dew claws to the hocks. Then insert leg spreader hooks, rope, or wire under these large tendons.

Secure the legs to a spreader, a short board, or a pipe. The rear legs should be held in a fully extended position. Attach the spreader, board, or pipe to ropes or chains and, with the aid of several friends or a block and tackle, hoist the carcass, head down, to a convenient working height. The carcass will remain in this upside-down suspended position for the remainder of the slaughter.

Using the same pulling-slicing technique and a sharp skinning knife, remove the hide from around the anus, down over the hips, and finally from the back. Sometimes a stout pulling and working the hide loose with your fingers will be all that is needed. Actually, the less you use the knife, the better, as your chance of nicking the meat is decreased.

Finally, remove the hide from the forelegs and neck. If you plan to save the head, skin down the face and remove the hide at the snout. If you don't want to use the head, remove it at the joint closest to the head with a sharp butcher knife and/or a meat saw. Discard the head in the garbage can set aside for waste.

Carcass suspended by rear-leg tendons. (Photo courtesy USDA)

Skinning the hams. The legs have already been skinned
and a cut has been made down the midline. (Photo courtesy USDA)

Remove the front feet at the joints by sawing through the bone. If you plan to save the feet, soak them in a bucket of ice water while you finish the slaughter. Otherwise, discard in the garbage can you have available for waste.

Continue the slaughter sequence (gutting and splitting) the same as you would after scalding/scraping.

You might want to try tanning the pigskin that you removed, but be aware that this is not an easy procedure for the beginner. Nonetheless, if you still want to tan your pigskin just for the experience, we recommend *Home Tanning & Leathercraft Simplified* by Kathy Kellogg (Williamson Publishing Co., Charlotte, Vt).

If you are tanning the hide, lay it out to cool, preferably on a concrete floor, while you complete the butchering. Otherwise, discard the skin with the other waste.

Scalding & Scraping

Scalding and scraping the hide, although preferred by most experts, is hard work. The most important consideration is maintaining an adequate supply of properly heated water. About 50 gallons of near-boiling water will be needed for a butcher-weight pig. Have the water ready before the animal is killed and bled. If the water is boiling in one 55-gallon barrel, it can be mixed with cold water in the scalding barrel to maintain the proper temperature. Also, you need to have available bell scrapers (available at livestock supply or tanning supply outlets) and dull butcher knives to remove the hair.

The animal can be scalded by several methods, but the easiest is to have two 55-gallon barrels available: one to heat water in and one to scald the hog in. Scalding temperatures between 140 and 145 degrees F. are best. Hair and the accumulated layer of oil, dirt, and outer skin cells (called *scurf*) will take 3 to 6 minutes to loosen at these optimal temperatures. Hair that is difficult to remove may require higher temperatures or longer scalding. About ¼ cup of lime added to the scalding water helps loosen the scurf and results in a whiter skin.

The risk of overscalding is not to be underestimated as it is often difficult to tell when scalding is enough and when it is too much. Overscalding causes the skin to contract around the base of the hair, "setting" it. Further, it cooks the skin. Hence, the hair and scurf become difficult, if not impossible, to remove.

Once you have the proper water temperature, lower the pig into the barrel, head first, and rotate the carcass, pulling it in and out occasionally (yes, this takes more than 1 person for a 200-plus pound hog!). Check the hair often. When it slips from the skin easily in the flank regions, remove the hog from the barrel and lower the rear of the hog into the water. Scrape as much of the hair from the face as possible while the rear end is scalding. When the hair slips from the rear flanks, remove the hog from the barrel and place on a concrete or wood slab or other convenient working place. Picnic tables have been used for scraping with some success.

Grip the legs with both hands and twist to pull off the hair. Then, remove the hair from the difficult areas first (head, feet, jowl) before proceeding to the easier ones (back, sides).

Scrape the hot carcass as quickly as possible with bell scrapers or dull knives because the skin tends to "set" as it cools. If patches are difficult to remove, cover them with burlap soaked in boiling water. When the hair is loosened, scrape again.

After most of the hair is removed, pour hot water over the carcass and continue scraping in a circular manner to remove any remaining scurf and hair. Use a sharp knife to remove hair that cannot be taken off with a scraper and dull knifes.

Although it might seem like a good idea to scald and scrape a second hog while the water is still hot before finishing the first, we don't recommend it. It is more important to get the first carcass prepared and chilled than to "waste" some heated water. Actually, we don't feel that anyone except an experienced butcher should even consider attempting more than 1 hog at a time. However, if you do plan to butcher 2 or more hogs, our suggestion is to keep the scalding water hot but not boiling while you finish the first carcass before you go on to the second.

Suspend the carcass by the rear leg tendons (see the details of this operation in the "Skinning" section earlier in this chapter). Once the animal is hanging, head down, a blowtorch can be used to singe off any remaining hairs, but be careful not to burn the skin. The carcass can be washed one more time at this point, too.

Evisceration (Gutting)

The slaughter sequence after skin or hair removal is the same for all large animals. If you have worked with a steer, sheep, or deer, you will already be familiar with this process.

Use a sharp boning or similar knife for these procedures.

Loosen the anus by cutting around it and pulling outward. Don't cut the large intestine. Tie the loosened anus with a piece of string to avoid contamination.

Remove the penis from a male hog by cutting through the skin along each side. Pull it upward and remove at its attachment at the base of the hams.

Cut between the hams, at their natural separation, through the connective tissue to the pelvic bone. Separate the hams by continuing the cut through the cartilage between the pelvic bones. A meat saw may be needed, especially for older animals.

Make a cut through the lean and fat from the neck to the top edge of the breastbone to open the chest cavity. Open the midline beginning where the pubic bone was split and continuing to the opening made at the chest. Keep the blade pointed outward to avoid cutting the intestines.

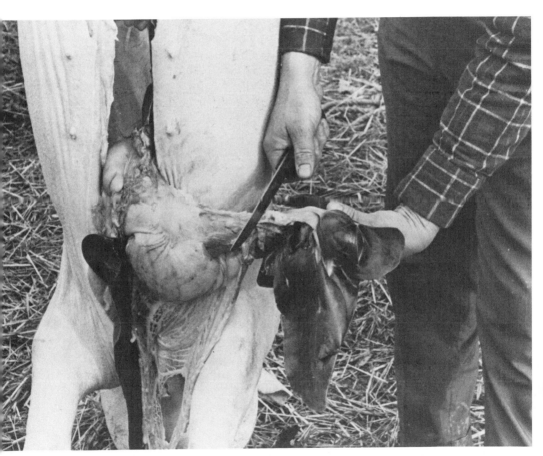

Removing the liver. (Photo courtesy USDA)

Allow the intestines and stomach to roll outward and hang. Do not let them fall because the esophagus will tear and spill its contents onto the carcass.

Pull the loosened large intestines down past the kidneys. Sever the attachments to the liver and remove the liver by pulling it outward and cutting the connective tissue. Remove the gall bladder, a small greenish-colored sack attached to the liver, by cutting part of the liver away beneath it and pulling the gall bladder and attached liver tissue away from the liver itself. Exercise extreme caution to avoid breaking the bile sack and allowing the contents to spill onto the liver. If the bladder should break and spill, the liver will be unfit for human consumption and must be discarded.

Pull the stomach and intestines outward and cut through the diaphragm, the thin sheet of tissue stretched across the bottom of the ribs. Pull the lungs outward and remove the heart. Cut down each side of the windpipe, severing the attachment to the head. Separate the heart from the lungs by cutting across the top. Split the heart open and wash thoroughly. Put the liver and heart in ice water to chill.

Splitting

Wash the inside of the carcass thoroughly with cold water to remove any clinging blood and to help cool the meat.

With a meat saw, begin splitting from the inside between the hams. Keep the split as near the center of the backbone as possible. Move around to the back if needed to saw through the shoulder and neck to the base of the head.

Remove the head at the joint closest to the head, leaving the jowls attached to the carcass. Remove the tongue, wash it, and place with the liver and heart. Save the head by soaking in ice water or discard it.

Remove the kidneys and the leaf fat from the inside of the carcass. Place the kidneys in ice water and save the fat for rendering. Then, wash the entire carcass thoroughly before chilling.

Now is a good time to examine the internal organs and the dressed carcass for any irregularities that might affect the fitness of the meat for food. A meat inspector is usually present to do this, but in a small farm situation, you become the inspector. Be particularly alert for bruises, parasites in the organs, enclosed abscesses, and tumors which can be easily removed if spotted. However, lung congestion, inflammation of any organ, and numerous abscesses or tumors should be viewed very seriously. Call a veterinarian to examine the carcass immediately.

Splitting the carcass. (Photo courtesy USDA)

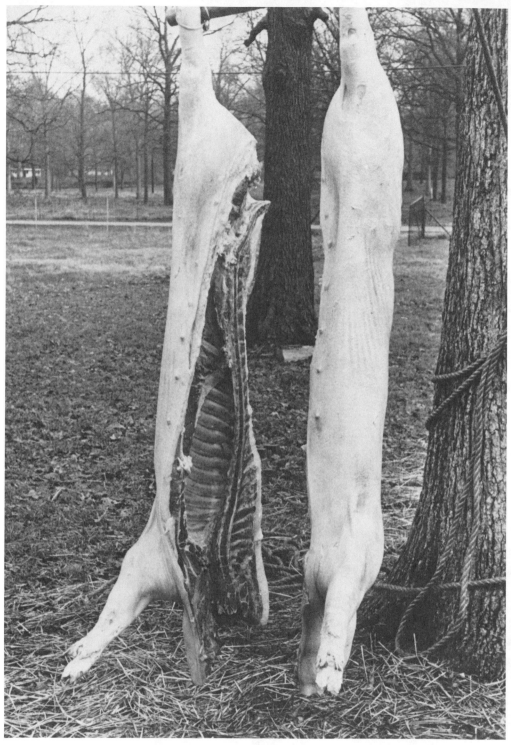

Sides of pork ready for chilling. (Photo courtesy USDA)

Chilling

Bacterial growth on the surfaces of a freshly slaughtered carcass can be slowed by prompt chilling. If the weather is suitable, wrap the carcass in a clean cotton sheet and hang in a well-ventilated shed or barn. The ideal cooling temperature is 28 to 40 degrees F. for 24 to 48 hours or until the entire carcass has cooled to about 35 degrees F. The best place to check for cooling is at the center of the hams.

Do not allow the meat to freeze before the 24 to 48 hour cooling time has elapsed or the meat will be tough. If prompt and thorough cooling is not possible on the farm, the carcass should be transported to a local locker plant for refrigeration.

Cutting the Carcass

After the carcass has cooled thoroughly, it can be cut and packaged for the freezer. The following equipment is recommended to do an adequate job: boning knife, large steak knife, steel, meat saw, freezer paper with tape, meat grinder. Additionally, you must have access to clean water.

Bear in mind that most home cuts probably will not resemble those you've seen in the market, especially if this is your first attempt at pork butchering. Nonetheless, the meat will taste the same no matter how it is cut.

The principal cuts will be the hams (back legs), the loin (along the backbone), the bacon and spareribs (stomach), the picnic and butt roasts (shoulders), and the jowl, neckbones, and specialty meats (especially the heart and liver). You might also want to save the feet, the tail (often used for greasing frying pans), the head, and tongue.

Begin by removing the hocks from the legs, then the legs from the body. If you will be curing or smoking the hams and/or shoulders, the hocks can be left attached.

Divide the remaining carcass into loin and belly with a straight cut from the edge of the tenderloin muscle on the ham end through a point on the first rib about 2 inches from the protruding edge of the split backbone. Remove the excess fat from the loin along the backbone to about a ¼ inch thickness. Slice the loin into roasts and chops. Since you are the butcher, you control how thick the chops should be and how large the roasts are. However, retail chops are ½ to 1 inch thick and roasts average ½ to ¾ pound per serving (about 3 pounds). Chops for stuffing are 2 ribs thick, which makes a pocket between the ribs.

Remove the neck bones from the shoulder by cutting beneath the ribs to the backbone and along each side of the vertebrae. Remove the jowl by a straight cut parallel to the cut that separated the shoulder from the side.

Divide the shoulder into roasts and steaks or leave whole. Separate the spareribs from the belly by cutting closely underneath the ribs beginning at the flank end of the ribs. Choice bacon is trimmed and squared.

Sausage

Sausage is made from the fat and lean trimmings produced from making roasts, hams, loins, and bacon. Ideally, sausage should be more than 50 percent lean, so save any extra fat for lard rendering. (See chapter 10 for sausage recipes.)

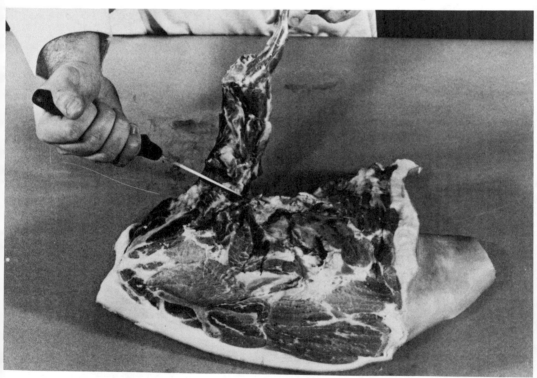

Removing neck bones. (Photo courtesy USDA)

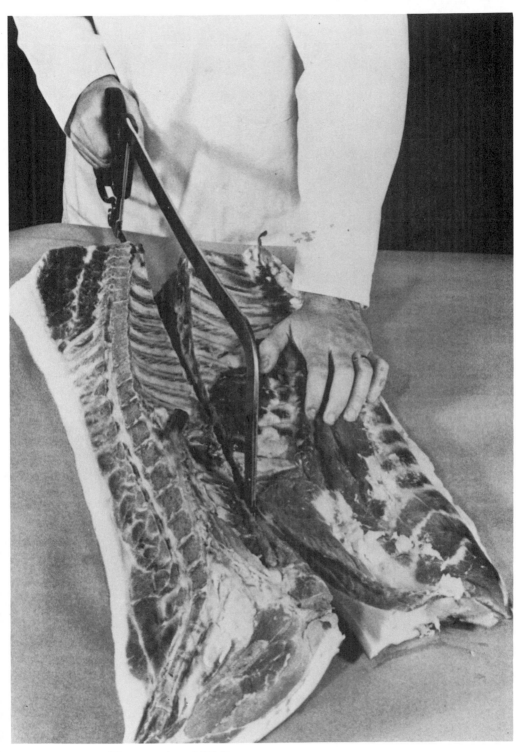

(Photo courtesy USDA)

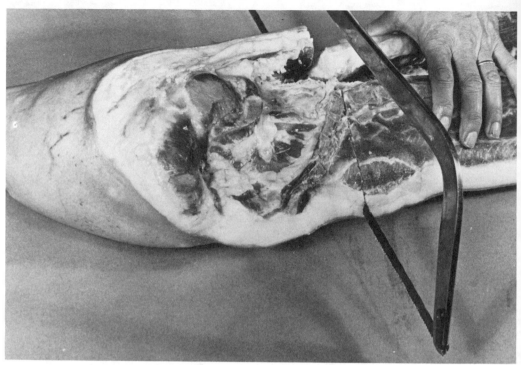

Removing the long ham. (Photo courtesy USDA)

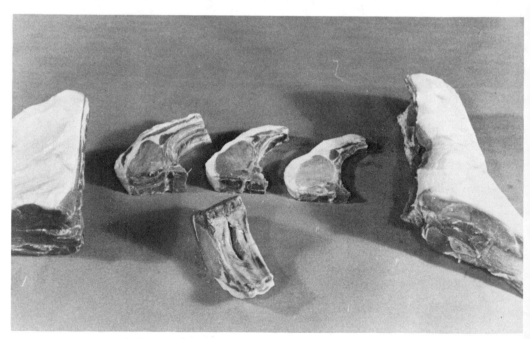

Loin roasts and chops. (Photo courtesy USDA)

STORAGE

Fresh pork should be wrapped properly and frozen quickly at 0 degrees F. or lower immediately after cutting. This is essential to maintain meat quality. Use wrapping materials specially designed for freezing, and package meat in convenient, family-sized portions.

With the pork cuts in the center of the wrapping material, bring the edges of the wrap together over pork and fold over at least twice. Wrap the meat tightly to eliminate as much air as possible. Double fold the ends toward the meat and fold under the package. Secure with freezer tape, and label and date each package properly.

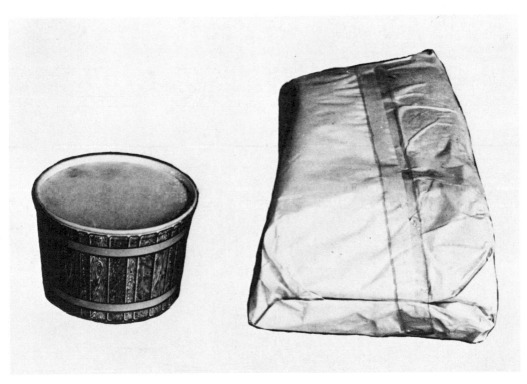

Wrapping the meat for the freezer.

Fresh pork will keep in the freezer for several months. We have had no problems with pork a year or more old, but most experts say that fresh sausage and variety meats should be used within 2 months, chops within 4, and roasts and fresh hams within 8.

Pork also can be canned, raw, in pint or quart jars using a pressure canner for 75 to 90 minutes at 10 pounds pressure. Canning is not a popular storage method because botulism (food poisoning) is a real possibility unless all equipment is kept very clean, the pressure canner is in perfect working order, and processing follows recommended times and temperatures exactly. The USDA offers a pamphlet, *Home Canning of Meat and Poultry*. If you want to try canned meats.

Chapter 10

PORK COOKERY

Pork roasts and chops, sausage and ham have had a prominent place on the American table for centuries. Originally, curing commonly was used to preserve the meat before refrigeration. However, today hams, bacon, and other pork cuts are cured simply for the flavor, and most will need to be frozen for long-term storage.

CURING PORK

Curing is the simple process of saturating meat fibers with preservatives such as salt and sugars. Nearly all curing and homemade sausage recipes also require a chemical called saltpeter, which is also known as nitrate/nitrite, to further enhance the preservation of the meat, as well as to give the pork its characteristic pink or reddish color. The presence of nitrate insures against the development of botulism (food poisoning) and also retards rancidity (oxidation of the fat). Nitrate is changed by bacterial action to nitrite.

The use of nitrates and nitrites in meat curing is currently being investigated by the USDA and the Food and Drug Administration. Nitrate/nitrite, like salt, can be toxic if eaten in large quantities. However, most of us would need to eat massive amounts of cured meat before we would reach these toxic levels. But another problem with nitrites is where the health concern arises. Nitrites combine with the natural breakdown product of proteins (amines) to form nitrosamines, some of which are known to cause cancer. Further, laboratory tests show that heating (cooking) cured meats increases the formation of nitrosamines, especially if the meat is well fried or burned as bacon occasionally is. What levels of nitrosamines are in cured meat products, how much is formed in the body after consumption, and what are the danger levels? Nobody knows the answers to those questions. People have been eating ham and other cured meats for generations using nitrate/nitrite preservatives, however the cancer connection has only recently been brought to light. Further, all plants and water from most natural wells contain nitrate/nitrites, so this isn't an uncommon chemical in our diet.

As with other recent health questions concerning pork, the final decision is the consumer's: consider the reported cancer risk versus the known risk of food poisoning when nitrate/nitrites are not used as a cured meat preservative.

There are basically 2 ways to cure meat: wet brine or dry cure. Both methods are used extensively for home curing, but the wet brine takes a bit longer and requires more equipment. However, according to most of the folks we've talked with, internal rotting of the meat is most likely to occur with the dry method. Other curers suggest that the dry cure is safer in warm temperatures. Nonetheless, if you follow the directions and take care that all the meat surfaces make contact with the curing chemicals, you should be successful with either method.

Wet Brine

This cure is enough for approximately 100 pounds of pork, which is about the maximum amount you want to work with at a time. If you have only 50 pounds, cut the recipe in half. If you have more than 100 pounds, freeze part of it to cure later.

Never mix the cure or hold the curing meat in a metal container. Curing chemicals react with the metal to produce an off-taste.

Place the chilled, trimmed meat cuts (ham, bacon, etc.) into a clean crock or barrel and cover with the following pickle recipe.

Wet Brine Pickle Recipe

- **8 pounds salt (noniodized pickling salt is preferred)**
- **2–3 pounds sugar (more sugar for a sweeter tasting ham; you can substitute brown sugar, molasses, or maple syrup for part or all of the sugar)**
- **2 ounces saltpeter or sodium nitrate**
- **4½ gallons water**

Weigh the meat down to keep it from floating. Also, cover the crock or barrel to prevent contaminants from falling in.

Keep the curing meat cold (36 to 40 degrees F.) during the curing period, which is about 4 days per pound (a 15-pound ham will take about 2 months). Every week, remove and reposition the meat so that surfaces which were previously in contact with other cuts are exposed to the curing solution.

If the meat temperature is too high, bacteria will multilply in the solution, causing a slimy growth on the meat. If this happens, discard the brine, wash the meat, and make a new batch of curing solution, reducing the salt in proportion to how much soaking time remains (for example, if half of the time remains, use half as much salt).

To speed curing, most commercial packers pump the brine into the meat with a tool that looks like a giant hypodermic syringe. The brine is injected into the ham to work from the inside out. Curing time is cut from weeks to a few days. In fact, some of the newer pumping methods are so effective that a full cure on a large ham can be achieved in less than a day.

If you can obtain a meat basting syringe or even a large medical-type unit, you might want to try the injection technique. However, timing of the cure will depend entirely on how thoroughly you saturate the ham fibers with brine. For safety sake, don't reduce the soaking time to less than 2 days per pound, even if you use brine injection.

Dry Cure

The dry cure method entails rubbing the meat with curing ingredients instead of soaking the meat in a solution. Dry-curing with only salt was once the most common method of preserving farm pork.

To try it yourself, use the same recipe ingredients that were listed with wet curing, but omit the water. The sugar (obviously molasses or maple syrup cannot substitute for sugar with the dry cure), salt, and nitrate should be mixed together thoroughly. Again, the recipe will cure 100 pounds of meat.

The cure will stick to the meat better if a thin layer of molasses or maple syrup is spread over the surface first. Then, rub the surfaces of the meat with the cure, paying particular attention to the crevices around the bone. Stack the cuts, skin side down in a cool room. Federal meat inspection regulations state that the temperature of the meat being dry cured should not get below 36 degrees F. or above 40 degrees F. during the process.

Curing meat should be placed in such a way that it can drain without sitting in the brine—try placing the curing cuts on stainless steel or plastic racks. Cover the meat with clean sheets or plastic wrap to prevent contamination from settling on it.

Bellies (bacon) usually need only 1 application of the salt mixture and commonly take about 7 days per inch of thickness to fully cure.

Hams and shoulders should be resalted with the curing mixture on the fifth day and will take 3 days per pound to fully cure.

After curing, soaking the meat will improve its quality and appearance. Soak in lukewarm water (not over 70 degrees F.) for approximately 2 minutes per day in the cure. (For example, if your meat cured for 15 days, soak the meat for 30 minutes.) Hang the meat to dry for 3 hours.

Supposedly, fully cured meat can be stored at room temperature. However, most meats routinely are frozen today. If you are a first-time curer, we suggest you freeze your meat. There is nothing more frustrating than cured meat kept at room temperature rotting from the inside out before Christmas dinner!

SMOKING PORK

Smoking cured pork improves the appearance and gives it a characteristic aroma and flavor. If you are smoking your meat at home, pay careful attention to the procedures to prevent spoilage and insect/rodent infestation.

Smokehouses

The building used to smoke meat can be as simple or elaborate as you want to design it. Minimally, it should be of reasonably tight construction to allow the regulation of temperature and air flow.

The smokehouse can be an old refrigerator, barrels, or large drums. Also, facilities are needed for making smoke and directing it into the smokehouse. If you intend to smoke large quantities of meat, consult your local extension agent for plans to construct a permanent smokehouse.

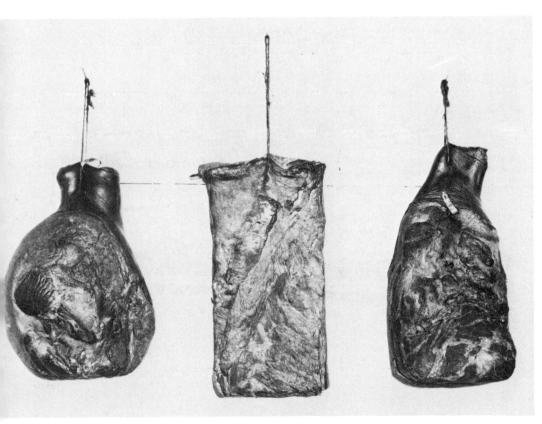

Meat cuts hanging in the smokehouse. (Photo courtesy USDA)

Smoking Process

All meat to be smoked should be soaked to remove the curing salt from the surface and then allowed to dry. We recommend soaking for 2 minutes per day of cure.

Hang the cuts in the smokehouse so that they do not touch each other or the walls. Use string or clean galvanized wire to hang the meat.

In a firepit, build a fire with hardwood such as hickory, oak, apple, or maple. Never use soft woods, such as pine, cedar, or spruce, which can deposit resins and turpentine-like chemicals on the meat, giving it a bitter flavor and a dark color.

Once the fire is burning, use damp hardwood sawdust to deaden the flame and produce smoke rather than heat.

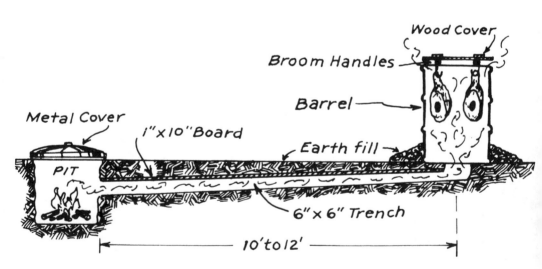

USDA suggested barrel smoker

The USDA suggests the following schedule for smoking cured hams:

1. **4 hours: Smokehouse temperature 120 degrees F. Damper open (pit cover open all the way) – smoke off (most of the smoke going into the air rather than the smokehouse).**
2. **6 hours: 140 degrees F. Damper one-quarter open – smoke on.**
3. **Raise the temperature to 170 degrees F. and hold until the meat reaches an internal temperature of 142 to 146 degrees F.**

   To be fully cooked, it is recommended that the cuts remain in the smokehouse until their internal temperature reaches 152 to 155 degrees F.

For smoking bacon, the following schedule can be used:

1. **2 hours: 115 degrees F. Damper open – smoke off.**
2. **2 hours: 130 degrees F. Damper closed – smoke on.**

   Raise the temperature to 140 degrees F. and hold until the internal temperature reaches 127 to 130 degrees F.

Cured, smoked meat can be handled several ways. It can be eaten immediately (a temptation, to be sure), refrigerated or frozen for future use, canned, or aged for that characteristic "country ham" flavor. Age meat at room temperature, 1 to 2 months for bacon, and 6 to 12 months for ham.

MAKING SAUSAGE

Sausage can be defined generally as chopped or ground meat and fat that has been blended with spices or other seasonings. In addition to salt, other flavorings such as peppers, allspice, anise, bay leaves, and cinnamon are used in sausage. Sodium nitrite is often added to inhibit the growth of food poisoning toxins.

Over 2,000 sausage processors annually produce over 5 billion pounds of more than 200 different kinds of sausage in the United States. While each commercial manufacturer and home producer has his or her own special formula and techniques, the general procedures are the same. The meat is ground or chopped and mixed into a batter with other ingredients. Then, the mixture is fried as patties or stuffed into casings and tied off into links. Depending on the end product desired, the sausage also may be cured, smoked, cooked, fermented, or dried.

An ordinary food processor usually isn't sturdy enough for sausage making. A special meat grinder with a coarse plate (½ inch holes) works best. After you add the salt and flavorings, regrind the mixture through a finer plate (⅛ inch to ¼ inch holes) for a more uniform mix of the seasoning.

Fresh sausage contains 20 to 30 percent fat. If more fat is used the sausage will shrink quite a bit during cooking.

SAUSAGE RECIPE #1

    100 pounds of pork trimmings (no more than ⅓ fat)
    2 pounds salt
    6 ounces pepper
    1–2 ounces powdered sage
    Optional: ground mace, nutmeg, cloves, or red pepper not to exceed 5 ounces

SAUSAGE RECIPE #2

    10 pounds ground pork trimmings, ⅓ fat
    10 teaspoons salt
    8 teaspoons ground sage
    4 teaspoons ground pepper
    2 teaspoons sugar
    1 teaspoon ground cloves

SAUSAGE RECIPE #3

    8 pounds ground pork trimmings, ⅓ fat
    10 teaspoons salt
    2 teaspoons sugar
    4 teaspoons ground pepper
    8 teaspoons ground sage
    Optional: 1 teaspoon ground cloves or 2 teaspoons ground nutmeg

Seasoned sausage can be frozen for up to 3 months. Unseasoned ground pork will freeze longer, up to 6 months. It can be seasoned and reground before using.

Preparing Sausage Casings From Intestines

Remove all the fat and membranes from the outside of the intestines. Turn them inside out. Clean the inside with borax water or undiluted chlorine bleach. Borax water can be prepared by dissolving 1 or 2 cups of powdered borax in a gallon of water.

Soak the intestines for 24 hours in the following solution: 1 ounce lime chloride in 1 gallon water. Scrape away the slime and inner lining to get the intestines as thin and transparent as possible. Wash carefully in clean water. Turn right-side out and wash again.

To stuff sausage into casings, you will need a special stuffing appliance or a lard press.

For larger sausages such as salami, suitable casings can be made from muslin or cheesecloth sewn into long bags. Dip the bags in water and wring them out before using. The old-fashioned way is to dip muslin bags into warm, melted, rendered lard before stuffing.

Hard Sausages

All hard sausages, such as pepperoni and salami, are stored at room temperature and must have a preservative agent such as saltpeter or sodium nitrate added to prevent food poisoning.

SALAMI

20 pounds beef chuck
20 pounds pork jowls and shoulder meat
10 pounds pork trimmings with some fat
1¾ pounds salt (noniodized pickling salt is preferred)
¾ pound brown or white sugar
½ ounce whole white pepper
¼ ounce saltpeter
¼ ounce garlic powder (or 2 pints crushed garlic cloves)

Grind the pork through a ¼ inch plate and the beef through a ⅛ inch plate. Mix all the meat ingredients thoroughly and spread on curing trays up to 3 inches thick. Use hardwood or porcelain for trays; anything else contributes an off-taste.

Thoroughly mix together the salt, sugar, and spices and sprinkle it over the meat. Let the meat and spice mixture set for 4 days at 38 to 42 degrees F. Remix the ingredients at least 3 times a day for the first 2 days and once a day for the last 2 days.

Stuff the mixture into casings. Lightly salt the outside after stuffing. Dry at 40 degrees F. with 60 percent relative humidity for 6 to 8 weeks. The secret to making good hard salami is in this drying stage. Too much humidity will cause molding, which can render the sausage inedible if not removed at once. If discovered early, mold can be scraped or wiped off without damage to the meat. To help prevent mold, wipe the outside of each sausage with vegetable oil.

PEPPERONI

14 pounds ground pork with some fat included
6 pounds ground beef
1¼ cups salt
2 tablespoons sugar
2 teaspoons saltpeter
1 tablespoon cayenne (red) pepper
6 tablespoons paprika
1 tablespoon anise seed
2 teaspoons garlic powder

Knead the spices into the ground meat. Spread the mixture no more than 3 inches deep on porcelain or hardwood trays. Cure at 38 degrees F. for 24 hours. Mix again and stuff into prepared casings. Hang at 48 degrees F. for 2 months until dry. Follow the recommendations for salami to prevent or remove mold.

USING THE LARD

To produce a high-quality lard with good stability, remove all the skin and lean meat from the back-fat and other fat trimmings. Cut the fat into small, uniform-size pieces. Fats from around internal organs yield a darker lard and should be rendered separately. Rendered leaf lard is very white and fine-textured and is considered the highest grade.

Next the lard is rendered to evaporate off all the water. Most experts agree that steam rendering is best because it eliminates the danger of scorching. The vast majority of packing house lard is steam rendered in a closed tank under steam pressure of 30 to 50 pounds and at a temperature of 285 degrees F. For the home cook, however, steam rendering requires the use of a pressure cooker and extreme diligence to prevent explosions. We recommend that you contact your local cooperative extension agent for advice before using this method.

Most homemade lard is rendered in an open kettle. Heat should be kept on low, and the fat must be stirred frequently to drive out all the moisture. The temperature of fat during rendering should be kept at 212 degrees F. if possible. As the water evaporates, the temperature will increase but do not allow it to go above 255 degrees F.

As the rendering process nears completion, *cracklings* (bits of browned skin and meat) will float to the surface. When they begin to settle to the bottom, the lard rendering is done.

For a whiter lard, drop in a few slices of peeled potatoes near the end of rendering to soak up any impurities. Traditionally, doughnuts are made in a kettle of freshly rendered lard before it is strained and cooled. We don't know if this tradition started as a way to draw impurities into the fried pastries or just because nothing tastes better than fresh doughnuts—with a large kettle of hot deep-frying fat available, why not?

Strain the lard through several thicknesses of cheesecloth and allow to cool, preferably at a temperature near freezing. While cooling, stir frequently to aerate and prevent graininess.

Containers should be filled to the top, sealed tightly, and stored in a dark place. Well-rendered lard will keep for a year at room temperature, longer if refrigerated.

Lard adds flavor and richness to foods when used as a shortening or for frying. It is especially useful for flaky, tender pastries and pie crust and for deep-frying.

HOMEMADE LARD PASTRY MIX

14 cups flour (bleached white flour will keep longer but unbleached or whole-grain flour can be used)

8 teaspoons salt

3½–4 cups lard

Mix the flour and salt well. Cut the lard into the flour mixture with a fork or pastry blender until crumbs are about the size of peas. Cover and store in the refrigerator until ready to use. This mixture will keep for about a month.

To make a 9-inch pie crust, add 2 to 4 tablespoons ice water to 1½ cups mix. Add the water, a small amount at a time, mixing quickly, until dough just holds a ball form. Roll to ⅛ inch thickness on a floured board and line pie pan. For a baked shell, prick the pastry evenly with a fork. Bake in a 450 degree F. oven for 8 to 10 minutes.

For a double crust pie, double the recipe.

Lard is also used for making soap. Recipes are usually available on a can of lye. The following method was a favorite in our family.

GRANDMA'S SOAP RECIPE

Mix 1 can lye in a quart of cold water. Use a large enamel or porcelain container. Stir carefully and thoroughly with a wooden spoon.

Slowly add the following:

4 pounds melted lard or other grease (lard works best)

3 tablespoons sugar

½ cup borax powder

⅔ cup ammonia

Do not use detergents or sudsing ammonia.

Slowly stir for about 1 hour or until the mixture begins to thicken. Then pour into 1 quart milk cartons or other paper cartons. Let stand for 24 hours in a cool place. Peel off the cartons and slice the soap into bars with a sharp knife. Place each bar in an old nylon stocking and hang in an airy place. Let the soap age and bleach for at least 3 months.

Grandma notes that it is good, shaved with a potato peeler, for laundry. She also suggests adding perfume and coloring if using it as hand soap.

SCRAPPLE

A favored Pennsylvania Dutch breakfast dish, scrapple is made from cooked pork and/or pork broth thickened with cornmeal and flour. The following recipes are traditional.

SCRAPPLE #1

4 pounds pork (neck bones, pigs' feet, other scraps or inexpensive cuts)

2 quarts water

2 cups yellow cornmeal

¼ cup finely chopped onion

1 tablespoon salt

1 teaspoon powdered sage

¼ teaspoon ground pepper

Cover the meat with the water in a large pan. Cover and simmer until the meat separates easily from the bones. Strain the meat from the broth. Discard the bones and grind the meat finely. Add water if necessary to bring the amount of broth to 8 cups and return to the pan. Add the cornmeal. Cook over medium heat until the mixture has the consistency of thick mush, about 5 minutes. Add the ground meat, onion, and seasonings. Pack into loaf pans that have been rinsed in cold water. Chill until firm. Remove the loaves from the pan.

To prepare immediately, slice the scrapple into ½-inch slices and pan fry in melted shortening until crisp and brown. Serve hot with maple syrup.

Scrapple will keep in the refrigerator for about a week. For longer storage, scrapple loaves can be wrapped in freezer paper or packed into freezer containers and frozen for up to a year.

SCRAPPLE #2

This recipe uses only pork broth and contains no meat.

1 cup coarse cereal grains (cornmeal is the most popular, but oats, whole wheat bulgur, or other grains can be substituted)
1 cup broth
Salt, pepper, sage, red pepper, minced onion, or other spices to taste

Add the cereal to broth. Bring to a boil to thicken. Add the spices and continue to cook until it achieves a porridge consistency. Pour into loaf pans. Chill until firm. To serve, slice and fry.

HEAD CHEESE

Split the head into halves with a meat saw. Remove the eyes and clean the ears and nostrils. Rub the head halves with coarse salt and pack loosely into a large kettle. Leave for 2 days in a cool place or refrigerate.

Wash the salted head in cold water and return to the kettle. Add the tongue, heart, and some lean trimmings if desired. Cover the meat with water and simmer until the meat is well done and will separate easily from the bones, about 3 hours. Remove the meat from the broth. Remove all the meat from the bones and cut it up finely. Discard the bones. Return the meat to the broth in the pan. Add seasonings as desired (salt, pepper, chopped onions, sage, or others according to taste) and simmer for 15 to 20 minutes, skimming off as much fat as possible and stirring occasionally. Pour into loaf pans or molds and chill. Head cheese can be eaten cold as sandwich meat or fried like scrapple. It will not hold together as well as scrapple because it lacks cereals.

STUFFED PIG'S STOMACH

Although the idea may not appeal to everyone, stuffed stomach is considered a delicacy in some parts of the country.

Start with a clean stomach. Wash thoroughly in cold water to remove all traces of food or other contaminants.

Combine the following ingredients to make the stuffing:

1 pound uncooked fresh sausage
8 large potatoes, peeled and cut into ½-inch cubes
1 tablespoon salt

Stuff into the stomach and sew up the openings. Place in a roasting pan with ¼ cup water. Cover and bake at 300 degrees F. for 3 hours. Uncover the pan for the last 30 minutes of baking.

OTHER VARIETY MEATS

Many parts of a hog can be eaten, although they are routinely tossed aside today.

Tongue can be simmered until tender with spices and/or vegetables. Tongue makes excellent sandwiches when chilled and sliced very thin.

Pigs' feet with the toes and dewclaws removed can be pickled.

The pig's tail is used for greasing frying pans and also can be deep-fried. This is considered a treat by some country kids we know.

Heart is cooked like tongue until tender. Liver is fried lightly and cooked on low until tender, about 10 to 12 minutes. Although many people don't like—or think they don't like—organ meat, it is delicious when prepared with some imagination. Further, heart and liver contain abundant vitamins and minerals and are nutritionally very dense.

ROASTING A WHOLE PIG

Although this idea may not appeal to everyone, a 40-pound to 100-pound pig can be roasted whole. Slaughtering is done the same as with the larger model, but since the "barbecue pig" is one-fourth to one-half the size, it is considerably easier to work with. In case you have forgotten, the slaughter sequence is kill, scald, scrape, and remove the intestines and other internal organs. Don't split the carcass. Leave the head in place, but remove the eyes.

Traditionally, the barbecue pig is roasted above hot coals on a homemade or commercial rotisserie. Be sure that your cooking source is hot coals, not flames, which could burn the outside before the inside is thoroughly cooked. Also, tie the pig to the rotating mechanism with more twine or wire than you think is needed. Once the pig cooks, the meat can slip from the rod unless painstakingly attached.

A meat thermometer will be necessary to show when the temperature at the thickest part of the hams reaches 170 degrees F. For a 50-pound pig, this may take as long as 12 hours.

The Hawaiian method of roasting a whole hog is to dig a pit, build a fire in it and let the fire die down to a good bed of coals.

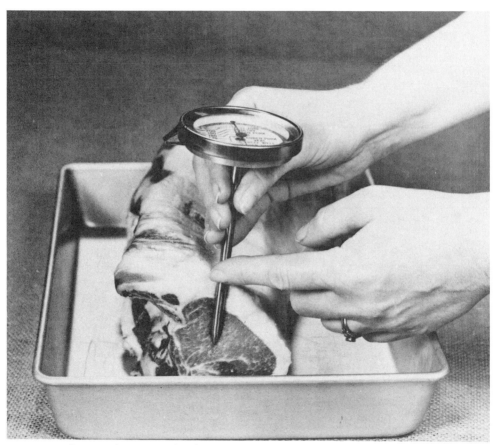

Proper placement of a thermometer in a pork roast.
(Photo courtesy USDA)

The slaughtered pig is wrapped in leaves (or aluminum foil) and buried in the coals, after which the pit is covered with dirt. It is hard to estimate when the pork is finished cooking. Without some experience, it's a lot of guesswork.

We tried the Hawaiian method once and a 75-pound hog took nearly 24 hours. However, we stuffed the pig with fruits and vegetables and this may be added to the time required. (By the way, it was delicious!) One suggestion we would like to make based on our whole-pig-roasting experience: Wrap the ready-to-cook hog in chicken wire whether using a rotisserie or a pit. You'll find that unless you have something like this to use as a "handle," removing a 20-pound to 80-pound chunk of hot pork from the coals without breaking it to pieces is nearly impossible.

Chapter 11

THE
NEXT STEP:
PRODUCING PIGLETS

Sooner or later in your pig-raising ventures a thought is going to cross your mind: "Why bother with the middle man (the farmer who raises the weaner pigs you buy)? How hard can it be to breed a sow and farrow a litter of piglets? I could sell some of the babies at weaner size, raise a couple to market weight for myself, and the whole system will be a snap . . . it'll pay for itself!"

Seductive as the idea may seem, don't you believe it! There's more to hog breeding than meets the eye. For example, consider these statistics: More health problems occur during the birth to weaning period than at any other time in a pig's life. The average producer loses one-fourth of the piglets before they are weaned, 65 percent of these before they are 4 days old, and 38 percent of that one-fourth are born dead. Then consider that each sow in a breeding herd requires over 2,000 pounds of feed a year and for all that feeding, 10 percent of the sows will fail to get pregnant. Then, consider the boar—sows don't have babies all by themselves!

At least 6 to 12 working sows are needed to justify the costs of keeping a boar who eats nearly as much per year as a sow and requires separate housing (most full-time hog-producing operations keep more than 50 sows). Bringing a boar into your farm for "stud servicing" (or taking your sow out) increases the risk of disease transmission—not to mention the potential problems caused by transporting the 500-pound-plus hogs to and from.

Keeping breeding stock and raising litters of piglets may seem simple, but it is costly and very risky. Your investment in terms of time, equipment, labor, housing, and skills required will be much greater than in a weaner-to-market operation. And the larger the scale of your hog production, the more you have invested, the greater will be your economic risks. You can expect breeding problems, farrowing (birth) problems, and many additional diseases to be concerned with. Further, the more hogs you raise per building, the greater the disease risk becomes. Then there's sales timing, which is critical. You must sell those weaned babies when the market is right for the whole operation to put a profit in your pocket. And, finally, you'll find that you need the experience not available in any book to expect a farrowing operation to be profitable.

We have been talking about raising a couple of feeder pigs for home pork in this book, and we cannot hope to completely cover a subject as complex and involved as hog breeding in one final chapter. Hence, although not designed for anyone serious about farrowing sows, this section will give a brief overview of the subject to satisfy your curiosity and direct you to more competent sources (a commercial raiser, your local veterinarian, or your county extension agent are some good places to look for help) should you decide in favor of starting from scratch.

We suggest that before trying to breed a gilt and raise a litter of piglets, you visit several local breeders. Most take pride in their animals and will give you the royal tour. This is your opportunity to ask questions about mating, gestation (pregnancy), farrowing (birth), castration, clipping needle teeth, tail docking, and any other matters you don't understand. Sometimes the raiser, seeing your sincere interest, will invite you to witness these operations. Often such an education will convince you for or against starting your own breeding herd.

Now we will take you on the journey through hog motherhood with a friend of ours: Ms. Piggy, that beautiful Hampshire-Yorkshire hog who farrowed our first litter of piglets.

MEET THE PARENTS: BOARS AND SOWS

A boar is sexually mature at 7 to 8 months of age and is considered fully mature by his first birthday. Full-grown boars can weigh as much as 1,000 pounds and each requires a separate pen and exercise area approximately ¼ acre in size. In no case should more than 3 young males be penned together (to prevent fighting). Some confinement operations give each boar an 8-foot by 8-foot pen with a 20-square-foot sleeping space and 2 feet of trough length.

Because boars are large and can be dangerous, most raisers routinely remove the tusks every 6 months.

Boars require 4 to 6 pounds of 14 percent feed and 2 to 5 gallons of fresh water per day. Younger boars who are still growing may need more.

A young boar under 1 year of age can service 1 sow daily or 7 weekly. A fully mature boar can double those figures. However, boars can experience temporary sterility lasting 6 to 8 weeks, which may be caused by stress, diseases (especially those causing an elevated temperature), or a hot summer environment. It is wise to consider some method of cooling in a hot climate to maintain the boar's virility.

Young female breeding stock up until their second pregnancy are referred to as *gilts*. Many young females show their first signs of *estrus* or heat by 9 months of age. However, stress of confinement or reproductive problems may delay this onset. Some gilts may *ovulate* (produce eggs), but will not show heat. After the first estrus, the female will come into heat every 18 to 24 days. The heat lasts 2 to 3 days. At this time, her vulva (external sex organs) will be swollen and reddish; she may have a discharge; and she will be restless, pacing and "barking." During the heat, the female is willing to be bred by the boar. However, most producers wait until the female is about a year old or at least until her third or fourth heat period before mating to increase the number of eggs produced.

Young, unbred (open) females may be penned together as long as there is sufficient sleeping, exercise, and trough space. Some producers keep all breeding females in separate pens, however. The stress of overcrowding causes many reproductive problems.

Gilts are fed 5 pounds of 16 percent protein feed per head per day until 10 to 14 days before breeding. At this time, the gilt is *flushed* to a high energy, high protein ration, 6 to 8 pounds per day.

This feeding schedule increases the ovulation (egg production) rate. Immediately after breeding, however, the females are switched back to 5 pounds of a 14 to 16 percent protein ration daily.

Limiting or equalizing the feed for a group of gilts and sows is difficult: some will eat too much, others won't get enough. Many producers recommend penning separately during the flushing to farrowing period so that feed intake can be closely monitored.

If you are serious about breeding hogs and raising piglets, you must be serious about your selection of parents. Pick the fastest-growing, leanest, soundest youngsters from large litters to begin with. Cull gilts and boars with physical problems and bad dispositions. Ideally, the boar should be sexually aggressive but docile around you. The sow should have large litters of uniform-size babies up to twice a year and her piglets should show fast growth rates and no disease symptoms. Herds can be improved by wise husbandry and sound breeding herd selections.

Sow with a litter of Yorkshire pigs. (Photo courtesy USDA)

MATING

Three basic mating systems with many variations are used today: pen-mating, hand-mating, and artificial insemination (AI). Only you can answer which is best for your situation. All three have been successful; all three have at times resulted in failure to conceive.

Pen-Mating

Pen-mating means placing the boar and several gilts or sows into the same pen. Boars may be rotated or the same male may be left in the pen continuously. Ten or fewer females per pen is the recommended ratio. The main advantage is that the labor requirement is minimized. However, this must be balanced against the disadvantages which include: spotty breeding (not all the females may be bred); not knowing breeding dates exactly, which leads to uncertain birth calculations; and, boars may be overworked, which could lead to illness or sterility.

Hand-Mating

Hand-mating means individually placing a gilt or sow in heat with a specific boar until mating is completed, then separating them again. This is usually repeated the next day as well. The main advantage is that mating is witnessed and the exact farrowing (birth) date can be calculated. Also, fertility of the boar is easy to check and breeding can be scheduled to occur at the optimum times, on the first and second day of estrus. The disadvantage is that extra labor is required to move the breeding animals between pens.

Artifical Insemination (AI)

Artificial insemination usually is only considered on specialized farms or by purebred breeders. The techniques and equipment necessary are readily available but tend to be expensive. Heat detection and timing are critical for successful AI. Also, some sperm do not survive the freezing/thawing conditions necessary and may result in smaller litters. However, the use of AI has the potential to control disease spread during mating and to genetically improve the herd. Also, the use of AI greatly reduces the number of boars necessary for a large sow herd. Labor is generally high with AI, even when properly designed facilities are available.

BREEDING MS. PIGGY

When we bred our 15-month-old gilt, Ms. Piggy, we went against expert advice and all the books and brought a boar to our farm for the mating.

Charlie was an extremely ugly, extremely large 6-year-old Yorkshire with an equally unbecoming disposition. Although he had an impressive breeding record, his appearance nearly changed our minds about using him as a mate for our beautiful Ms. Piggy.

Charlie came from a small farm with a small pen not much bigger than he was and he moved readily in on Ms. Piggy's roomy barn stall and exercise yard. Although our gilt got pushed around some

Meet Ms. Piggy, our beautiful Hampshire/Yorkshire hog who farrowed our first and only litter.

when Charlie adopted the hay bedding and the feed trough, she was in heat and so she let him take charge.

Charlie's 3-day visit turned into a 2-week stay when his owner continually procrastinated about the pick-up time. Our "free" mating service was costing a fortune in extra feed! Finally, much to our and Ms. Piggy's relief, Charlie was scheduled to return home. Actually, it wasn't easy to convince him to leave. Several hours of pushing, bribing, and frustration were required before Charlie was securely loaded into the truck.

Two days later, we learned that old, ugly Charlie had not been happy in the restricted pen on the small farm back home. Apparently spoiled by his visit with Ms. Piggy, Charlie decided that he wanted more—more freedom and more food. He walked through his electric fence and wood shelter without a grunt, not slowing for a minute. At first he headed straight for the feed room where he consumed 80 pounds of corn. Then, off he trotted toward the next farm down the road.

Charlie died that day of a "lead overdose" when his owner decided shooting him was easier than trying to convince him to return home. Charlie became a memory and an excellent batch of pepperoni sausage!

GESTATION

Hog pregnancy (gestation) lasts for 3 months, 3 weeks, and 3 days or an average of 114 days. Sadly to report, the only sure method of pregnancy detection in the bred female is still birth. Some experts say that if a heat period does not occur 18 to 24 days after breeding, you can assume that the female is pregnant. However, an occasional gilt or sow will experience an "artifical pregnancy" and will be unbred but without detectable heats. Hence, you may be feeding a supposedly bred female for almost 4 months only to find that she wasn't in the motherly way at all.

Pregnancy diagnosis with ultrasonic detectors is supposed to be 90 to 95 percent accurate a month after breeding, but a producer would need to farrow 300 litters a year for 2 years to pay for the equipment.

We'll assume that your female did indeed become pregnant when she was mated. What should you do now? Stay calm. Most females have no problems with pregnancy. However, excessive feed intake may result in a reduced number of babies born alive. So cut back on the pregnant female's feed ration to 4 to 6 pounds of

14 percent feed daily. You can placate her with high-fiber additions to her diet such as pasture, alfalfa, hay, and wheat straw. Gilts will gain 75 to 100 pounds and sows will add 50 to 70 pounds during pregnancy.

The heaviest losses of fertilized eggs occur during the first 10 days after mating, and the most critical period for an aborted pregnancy is between the 18th and the 32nd day. If a pregnancy will be lost, it will be during this first month. These losses are no worse than those experienced by other mammals, and at present, the causes of early pregnancy failures are unknown. However, you can lessen the

Ms. Piggy in her nest.

risks of an aborted pregnancy by starting with sound genetic parents and providing the best possible environment for the pregnant female.

Eventually, pregnant animals will begin to show outward signs of pregnancy. The most obvious are an enlarged abdomen and the developing mammary glands. Most pregnant females can be identified as being *piggy* (a pig-raiser's term meaning pregnant) by 80 days. A few exceptional mothers show no signs of pregnancy but still deliver several healthy babies and a few others show all the signs but have none.

FARROWING

Approximately 24 to 48 hours before birth is anticipated, the soon-to-be mother will begin a restless stage of trying to build a nest in preparation for her babies. Her udders will be full of milk which can be squirted out if squeezed. At this time, most producers move the expectant mother to a farrowing unit where she is washed and disinfected. This area has a 55-degree F. temperature for the mother and a 90-degree to 95-degree F. area for the newborn babies who are easily chilled (after the first few days, the nursery temperature can be reduced to 70 to 80 degrees F.).

Farrowing crates and pens have the advantages of saving space and bedding, being easy to clean and disinfect, offering less opportunity for the mother to lay on her young, and facilitating the taking of temperatures, giving injections, etc. Their disadvantages are that they inhibit the mother's natural nest-building tendencies, they restrict her exercise, and they limit the chances of the piglets learning things like eating, cleanliness, rooting, etc. from their mother.

When Ms. Piggy had her litter, we decided to go against all the books and let her do it naturally. We gave her a relatively clean pen with plenty of clean straw and access to the exercise yard and water. We have to admit, it was very rewarding watching her chop the straw into small bits with her teeth before piling it up into a beautiful nest. She worked on that bedroom for hours before collapsing in the center in complete exhaustion. We waited several more hours, rubbing her enlarged belly and full udders, but no babies arrived, so we went about our other business and left her to her nest.

Labor usually begins within 24 hours after the nest-building activity begins. At first, the mother's respiration rate and temperature will increase. Then abdominal contractions will begin. When small amounts of blood and mucus are discharged, birth should begin within an hour or two.

We missed Ms. Piggy's birthings. We sent one of our children to the barn to check on her several hours after she had built her nest. When he returned, he looked at us quite matter-of-factly and reported, "Yup. She had babies!" We raced to the barn to find that Ms. Piggy had 6 fine piglets who were already rooting around in the hay and sucking quite happily on her swollen teats. Ms. Piggy was obviously too tired to talk much (except for a few faint grunts,

Ms. Piggy had 6 fine babies.

mostly to her offspring rather than to us), so we removed the after-birth and left her with her new family.

Labor usually lasts 30 minutes to 5 hours with approximately 15 minutes between birthings. The afterbirth, tissues from the placenta which nourished the piglets during pregnancy, is delivered after all the babies have arrived. It should be removed and disposed of.

Prolonged labor is associated with overweight mothers, genetic problems, and babies caught in the birth canal. Most experts agree that someone should be on hand if difficulties are experienced. Manual assistance with a well-lubricated, gloved hand or a drug to speed up labor (oxytocin) may be necessary. Most mothers in labor are oblivious to the world. Some, however, are hysterical and vicious. These should be culled.

Piglets are born wet and covered by a thin membrane. Most will dry quickly, especially in warm weather or under a heat lamp without any attention whatever. However, some farmers insist on wiping each baby clean as it is born. Most of the time, this is unnecessary, but it doesn't hurt the baby, either. Sometimes, however, the mucus and membranes may inhibit the piglet's breathing. Then, manual removal of any impeding substances is suggested. For this reason, presence at birth reduces the number of stillborn babies.

Most breeders remove the piglets from the mother after all are born to prevent the mother from accidentally crushing them and to weigh, identify, and examine each newborn pig. They also clip the needle teeth by ½ inch and dip the umbilical cords in an iodine solution to prevent possible infection. We did none of this and had no problems. But maybe we were just lucky.

Teeth clipping to prevent nipple injury to the nursing mother is done with wire cutters. Care must be taken or the babies' teeth could crack or the gums be injured which might lead to infection.

Each baby must receive the "first milk" or *colostrum* to be protected temporarily against common, local bacterial infections by the antibodies in the sow's milk. The average litter size is 10 to 12, with 14 apparently being the biological maximum, and usually the mother has sufficient nipples for her infants. However, extra or orphaned babies can be fostered to another sow before they are 3 days old to get enough colostrum.

The teats closest to the mother's head give the most milk, and these are usually claimed by the largest, most aggressive youngsters. The runts and weaklings are often left with a "hind tit." Although 60 percent of the runts born weighing less than 2 pounds die, good results can be achieved with supplemental bottle feeding—but not often. Most runts are doomed to die or remain runts despite all your efforts on their behalf.

MANAGING BABY PIGLETS

During *lactation* (milking), sows should be fed as much as they will eat to obtain maximum milk production. A sow will normally consume 9 to 15 pounds of 14 percent protein feed per day. It is also recommended that milking sows be kept in a 60-degree to 70-degree F. environment for the best milk production. However, if the temperature goes above 70-degrees, the sow's feed intake will be reduced.

Most experts agree that baby pigs need access to a heat source (70 to 80 degrees F.) for at least the first 2 weeks of their lives. Although we offered a special heated corner to Ms. Piggy's babies, they still preferred to snuggle up to mother when it got chilly.

Ms. Piggy's babies learned quickly about the world outside.

Experienced farmers also suggest that if a farrowing crate isn't used, some sort of railing should be attached to the pen to give the piglets an escape route from the sow when she lays down. All too often, unsuspecting little ones are crushed under the weight of their own mother. This is called *overlaying*. We ignored this advice, too, and all of Ms. Piggy's babies survived. However, she made such a deep nest of chopped straw that even when a little one was caught below her as she plopped down, he could scramble back up under her through the bedding.

Early in their lives, piglets are routinely subjected to the ordeals of tail docking, especially in confinement and crowded conditions, ear notching for identification, and castration of male market pigs. None of these procedures are particularly painful for the young pigs, but their screaming may upset the mother. Most raisers take the babies to another area out of the mother's hearing range.

Castration

Castration is best done early in the piglet's life. It is much easier then. Further, if the castrated youngster is put into a clean pen with his mother, the incisions will heal faster with less risk of infection. Plan to have an assistant on hand for castration day, as 1 person normally holds the piglet upside-down while another performs the actual operation.

Some raisers have had success castrating small piglets while they were laying in a V-shaped trough, but pigs squirm and jump. To insure that cuts are placed only where you want them, the two person method is most reliable. Also, seek help from your veterinarian or an experienced hog farmer if you haven't done this before.

Tail Docking

Tail docking does not require removal of the entire tail, but merely the least sensitive tip. This is done with wire cutters or a similar tool. If the tail is not manually shortened, the piglet's littermates often will chew it off. Docking carries less risk of infection than biting.

Ear Notching

Ear notching or some other form of identification of the litter is essential if you run an extensive breeding operation. Usually it is accomplished immediately after birth when the records are being filled out.

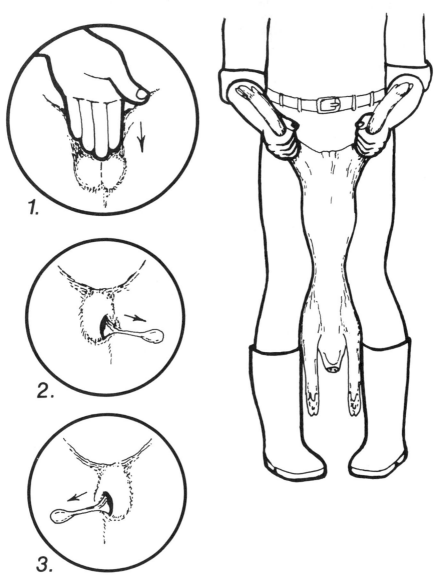

Castration procedure. An assistant holds the piglet up-
side down, holding the hind legs and bracing the pig
with his/her knees. The procedure is
1. Push testicles forward and make an incision.
2. Pull the testicles and tunic (white membrane) out
   until it snaps off.
3. Repeat with the second testicle. Paint the wound
   with antiseptic.

Small-scale raisers with 4 or fewer hogs normally do not tattoo or notch the animals' ears because they know which pig is which. If, however, litters are produced for sale regularly, identification is important. Breeders' associations (see Appendix C) can provide accepted ear notching systems.

Feeding

Before her babies were even a few days old, Ms. Piggy took them all outside to introduce them to the soil, the mudhole she had created near the water trough, and where dinner was served. Because she only had 6 youngsters and 12 functioning teats, the piglets grew fast. We loved to go to the pen and watch them scamper about squealing at each other and any stray chickens who wandered into their area. Ms. Piggy was a devoted mother. A squeal of fear or pain from one of her babies brought her running with a stern bark to see what was the problem.

Piglets can begin eating a starter mash as young as a week or two old. A 20 percent protein prestarter ration is suggested; however, you must find a feeding area that mother can't reach or she will gobble down the goodies leaving little for her babies. Feeding piglets out of reach of the sow is called *creep feeding*. The sooner the babies begin getting substantial nutrition from food other than mother's milk, the easier it will be to wean them entirely.

Baby pigs need iron supplements within a few days of birth because the sow's milk does not contain enough to prevent them from developing *anemia*. If the babies are raised with access to the outdoors, they will instinctively get the iron they need from the soil. However, most litters are kept in confinement and must be given iron by injection or orally. We gave Ms. Piggy's babies oral iron (they loved it) although they probably got plenty from the soil in their pen. Another way to provide iron for confined piglets is to throw clean sod or dirt to them at least 2 or 3 times a week. The iron solution also can be painted on the sow's udders, if she will allow you to do it.

Piglets can nurse for up to 3 months although most commercial raisers wean early (at 3 to 6 weeks of age) to get the sow bred and into production again (a sow won't come into heat while nursing). Milk flow averages 1 to 1½ gallons a day after farrowing and peaks at 2 to 2½ gallons a day a month later. Milk flow, however, is affected by many factors such as stress, diet, size of litter, diseases, and environment.

Weaning is traumatic for mother and babies no matter when it is done. The younger the piglets, the worse it is on them. Eight weeks is the average weaning age. Only wean babies who weigh more than 12 pounds and wean the largest pigs first, leaving the smaller ones with mother until their sizes increase a bit. After weaning and up until marketing size (25 to 40 pounds) feed the young pigs an 18 percent protein starter menu.

And now you're back to where we started: feeder pigs ready to be raised for your own pork or sold to other farmers. We're sure that we made the breeding-farrowing operation sound easier than it really is. Although watching this miracle of nature was satisfying, we concluded that motherhood just required too much of our time. These days, we've gone back to raising our porkers from weaner to market size only.

Appendix A

HOG HOUSING: CONSTRUCTION IDEAS

Building a pig shelter from scratch does not have to be an awesome task similar to constructing a barn. If, like us, you raise only 2 or 3 hogs a year, only during the warm months, your shelter needs are considerably less complicated than those of the commercial raiser who has several hundred head of swine to house year-round.

In this section of the book, we will give you some small-scale building ideas, as well as a quick look at large-scale, commercial construction types. We don't expect you to need the latter information, but we have included it for your pig-raiser's knowledge.

SMALL-SCALE HOG SHELTERS

If you live in a very warm climate and your hogs are penned in a pasture area or a land-clearing lot, chances are good that the only housing they will require during the spring to fall period is a frame with a roof. Your main objective will be to provide shade, because hogs are quite susceptible to heat stroke.

A simple 3-sided shelter that provides shade and protection from drafts is sufficient in warm weather.

Even if your mildest weather is a little cooler, a 3-sided shelter with a roof for shade and draft protection is usually sufficient.

Many hog raisers prefer an A-frame shelter. It makes efficient use of materials, is warm and draft-free for cool climates, and is easy to move from pen to pen if needed. An A-frame can be as simple or as complex as you make it. We've raised hogs with 3-sided A-frames that lacked even a floor and we've had no problems. However, this type of structure can be designed with doors, ventilation windows, complete floors, and skids for moving.

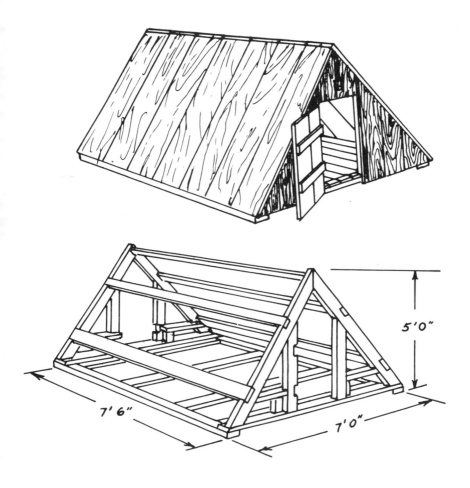

A-frames can provide easily built shelter. For warm, dry weather shelter, omit the door and the floor.

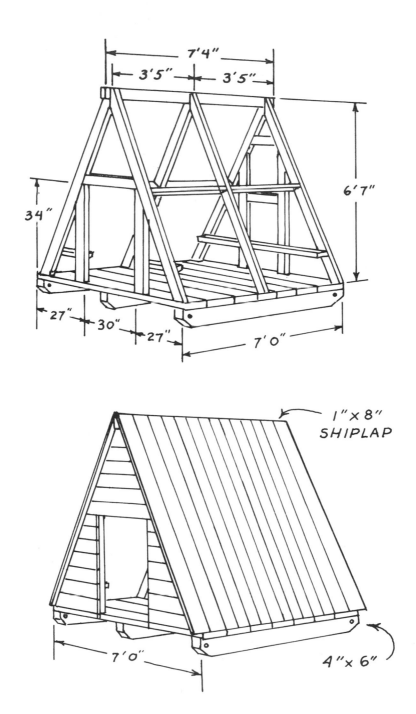

7'4"

3'5"   3'5"

6'7"

34"

27"   30"   27"   7'0"

1"×8"
SHIPLAP

7'0"

4"×6"

A more complicated A-frame shelter on skids.

Like A-frames, shed-type structures are both popular and flexible. The slightly slanting roof allows for rain drainage, skids can be added for portability, and the structures can have 3 or 4 sides. Although optional in dry climates, floors are recommended when the weather is wet and rainy.

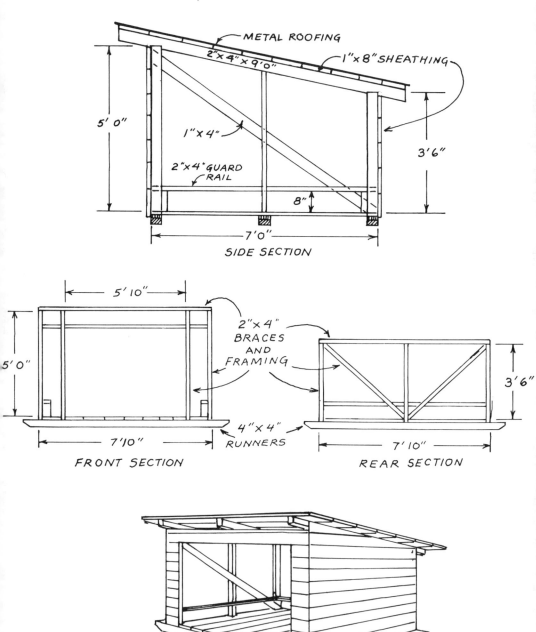

Shed shelter on skids.

THE TRUCK CANOPY HOG HOUSE

One year, we got to thinking that the wooden canopy we made for our pick-up truck might make an excellent hog house. We needed a new pig shelter anyway. Although the canopy was only meant to be temporary, it worked so well that we decided to include plans for its construction.

The nice part about the canopy house is that during the winter when we have no pigs, the house goes back on the truck (we have a small import truck, but this idea will work with any model). Then, in March or April, the piglets are brought to the farm in the truck, the canopy comes off, and 2 people and a handcart can move the canopy house to the selected pigpen area. Ta da! Instant shelter!

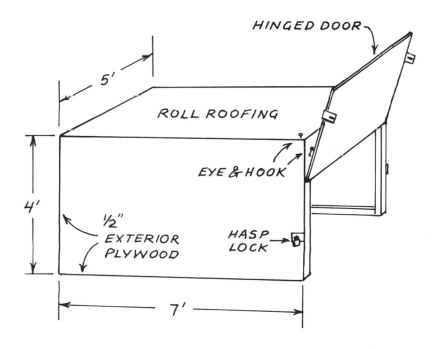

SEE NEXT PAGE

This canopy house can be altered to fit any truck bed size. This house is waterproof, warm, draft-free, and should work well in areas where a dirt floor is sufficient. We bed the inside well with straw when it is being used as a pig shelter. When moving the canopy around, shut and secure the door. At this writing, the canopy house has lasted through 2 winters on the truck and 2 summers with hogs—and it is still going strong!

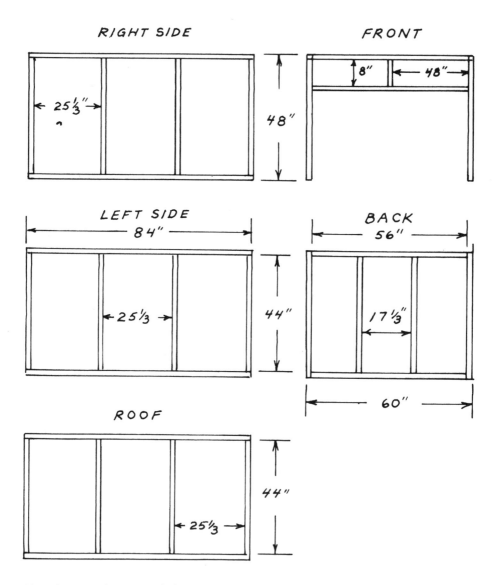

Plans for a truck canopy shelter.

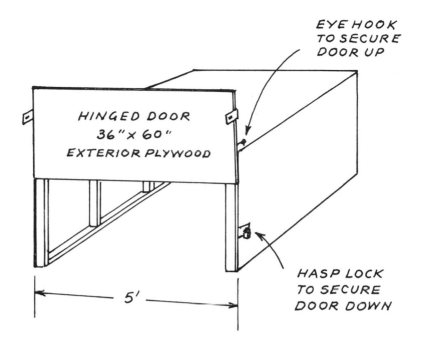

EYE HOOK
TO SECURE
DOOR UP

HINGED DOOR
36" x 60"
EXTERIOR PLYWOOD

HASP LOCK
TO SECURE
DOOR DOWN

5'

THE TRUCK CANOPY HOG HOUSE

Materials List

(4) 2-inch by 2-inch by 84-inch studs
(10) 2-inch by 2-inch by 44-inch studs
(6) 2-inch by 2-inch by 56-inch studs
(1) 2-inch by 2-inch by 8-inch stud
Exterior ½ inch plywood sections:
     (Front) 36-inch by 60-inch
     12-inch by 60-inch
     (Back) 48-inch by 56-inch
     (Sides) (2) 48-inch by 85-inch
     (Roof) 48-inch by 86-inch
     13-inch by 85-inch
14 feet composition roll roofing
¼-pound ½-inch roofing nails
½-pound 10d nails
½-gallon roofing cement
(2) hasps and locks (to secure door down)
(2) large hooks and eyes (to secure door up)
Roof and side panel are 1 inch longer than studs to match seams.
Paint for exterior (optional)

LARGE-SCALE BUILDINGS

Confinement and modified confinement buildings are not something the small-scale, 2- or 3-hog, part-of-the-year farmer should even consider. As this illustration shows, confinement buildings are very complex and very expensive to construct.

However, if you find that raising hogs is something you enjoy so much that you'd like to expand to a full-time, large-scale hog operation, this diagram will give you some perspective.

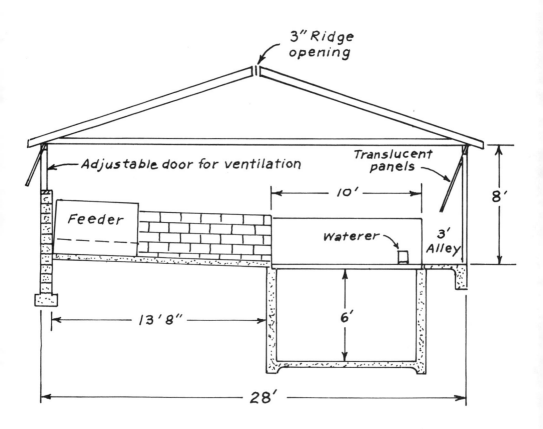

Suggested confinement building for growing-finishing operation.

Appendix B

GLOSSARY

ABATTOIR Commercial butcher or slaughterhouse.

BARBECUE PIG Swine usually under 100 pounds to be cooked whole.

BARROW A male hog castrated at a young age and destined for pork production.

BOAR Sexually mature male hog.

CHUFFY Lard-type hogs; very plump and fatty.

CRACKLINGS Bits of browned meat and skin that are removed when rendering lard.

FARROW Swine terminology for giving birth.

FEEDER PIG Swine weighing 25 to 220 pounds.

FLUSHING Increasing feed prior to breeding a female to increase the number of eggs shed and the size of the litter farrowed.

GILT Young female swine selected to breed.

HETEROSIS See HYBRID VIGOR.

HYBRID VIGOR The result of crossbreeding; offspring grow faster and show better feed efficiency than purebred parents.

LARD Rendered hog fat.

LOP EARS Forward-flopping ears, sometimes nearly covering the eyes.

MARKET HOG Swine ready for butcher at about 220 pounds.

MASTING Running swine through a forest in the autumn to eat nuts and seeds.

OVERLAYING Sow crushes and kills her babies when laying down.

OXYTOCIN A hormone which causes smooth muscle contractions; stimulates uterine contractions and aids in birth. Also helps cause milk letdown after birth.

PASTEURELLOSIS	See SHIPPING FEVER.
PROLIFICACY	The number of piglets produced (born alive) by a sow.
PSS	Porcine Stress Syndrome. See SHIPPING FEVER.
RANGY	Usually refers to wild meat. Lean, but stringy and tough.
RENDER	Heating fat to drive out moisture and remove impurities. Improves keeping and cooking qualities.
SALTPETER	Potassium nitrate. See SODIUM NITRATE/NITRITE.
SCURF	Outermost hog skin layer containing oil, dirt, and skin cells. Removed with hair when scalding and scraping during slaughter.
SHIPPING FEVER	A set of flu or pneumonia-like symptoms that is usually caused by the stress of transporting.
SHOAT	See WEANER PIG.
SODIUM NITRATE/ NITRITE	Chemical added to cured meat products to prevent food poisoning and improve flavor and color.
SOFT PORK	Meat that remains soft, flabby, and oily even under refrigeration. Usually caused by feeding unsaturated fats and oils before butcher.
SOW	Older female swine who has given birth to 1 or more litters.
SPF	Specific Pathogen Free hog who was born by caesarean section in a sterile environment.
STAG	Boar that is castrated after maturity.
SWINE	Generic term for all pigs and hogs of every kind, sex, and age group.
TRICHINOSIS	Parasitic disease caused by a microscopic nematode worm.
WALLOW	A deep water or mud hole created by or for hogs and used for cooling and skin parasite control.
WEANER PIG	Swine weighing 25 to 40 pounds.

Appendix C

SOURCES FOR MORE INFORMATION

BOOKS: SUGGESTED READING AND BIBLIOGRAPHY

Jerome D. Belanger, *Raising the Homestead Hog* (Emmaus, Penn.: Rodale Press, 1977).

Jerome D. Belanger, *The Homesteader's Handbook to Raising Small Livestock* (Emmaus, Penn.: Rodale Press, 1974).

Richard A. Battaglia and Vernon B. Mayrose, *Handbook of Livestock Management Techniques* (Minneapolis, Minn.: Burgess Publishing Co., 1981).

W. E. Carroll, et. al., *Swine Production* (New York, N.Y.: McGraw-Hill Book Co., 1962).

Editors, Countryside Magazine, *Raising Animals for Fun & Profit* (Blue Ridge Summit, Penn.: Tab Books, Inc., 1984).

Albert J. Davis and Robert R. Schubert, *Alternative Natural Energy Sources in Building Design* (New York, N.Y.: Van Nostrand Reinhold, 1974).

M. E. Ensminger, *Swine Science* (Danville, Ill.: The Interstate Printers & Publishers, Inc., 1970).

M. E. Ensminger, *The Stockman's Handbook* (Danville, Ill.: The Interstate Printers & Publishers, Inc., 1978).

Elwood M. Juergenson, *Handbook of Livestock Equipment* (Danville, Ill.: The Interstate Printer & Publishers, Inc., 1971).

Kathy Kellogg, *Home Tanning & Leathercraft Simplified* (Charlotte, Vt.: Williamson Publishing, 1984).

Jim Leckie, Gil Masters, Harry Whitehouse, and Lily Young, *Other Homes & Garbage: Designs for Self-Sufficient Living* (San Francisco, Calif.: Sierra Club Books, 1975).

The Mother Earth News, *Handbook of Homemade Power* (New York, N.Y.: Bantam Books, 1974).

Staff, Organic Gardening Magazine, *Organic Gardening* (Emmaus, Penn.: Rodale Press, 1978).

Louise Sherman Schoon and Corrine Hardesty, *The Complete Pork Cookbook* (New York, N.Y.: Stein and Day, 1977).

Jack Denton Scott and Ozzie Sweet, *The Book of the Pig* (New York, N.Y.: G.P. Putnam's Sons, 1981).

Jack Sleight and Raymond Hull, *Homebook of Smoke-Cooking Meat, Fish, and Game* (Harrisburg, Penn.: Stackpole Books, 1977).

C. E. Spaulding, D.V.M., *A Veterinary Guide for Animal Owners* (Emmaus, Penn.: Rodale Press, 1976).

Carol H. Stoner, ed., *Producing Your Own Power* (New York, N.Y.: Vintage Books, 1974).

SMALL-SCALE FARMING MAGAZINES

Blair & Ketchum's *Country Journal*. Monthly. $15.00/year. Subscription information: P.O. Box 2405, Boulder, CO 80322

Countryside. Monthly. $15.00/year. Subscription information: 312 Portland Road, Waterloo, WI 53594

Farm & Ranch Living. Monthly. $11.95/year. Subscription information: Reiman Publications, P.O. Box 475, Wilwaukee, WI 53201

Farmstead. Bi-monthly. $15.00/year. Subscription information: The Farmstead Press, Box 111, Freedom, ME 04941

The Mother Earth News. Monthly. $18.00/year. Subscription information: P.O. Box 70, Hendersonville, NC 28791

HOG-RAISING PERIODICALS

Hampshire Herdsman. Monthly. $5.00/year. Subscription information: Hampshire Swine Registry, 1111 Main Street, Peoria, IL 61606

National Hog Farmer. Monthly. $15.00/year. Subscription information: The Webb Company, 1999 Shepard Road, St. Paul, MN 55116

Pork Challenger. Quarterly. Subscription information: The National Pork Producers Council, P.O. Box 10383, Des Moines, IA 50306

The Yorkshire Journal. Monthly. $10.00/year. Subscription information: P.O. Box 2417, West Lafayette, IN 47906

FOR MORE INFORMATION

The American Meat Institute (P.O. Box 3556, Washington, D.C. 20007 or 1700 North Moore St., Arlington, VA 22209, (703) 841-2400) has the following pamphlets free for the asking. This organization can also provide answers to your questions about meat.

- **What's in the Meat We Eat?**
- **Give Breakfast a Break**
- **Brown Bagger**

Breeders Associations

These organizations can help you locate hog raisers in your area by providing a list of registered breeders. They also have available for the asking several publications about their breeds, registration requirements, and other useful hog-raising information.

- **American Berkshire Association, P.O. Box 647, Lebanon, IN 46052-0647. (317) 482-3042**

- **American Landrace Association (Same address and phone number as the American Berkshire Association)**

- **Chester White Association, P.O. Box 228, Rochester, IN 46975. (219) 223-3512**

- **Poland China Record Association, P.O. Box B, Knoxville, IL 61448. (309) 289-6786**

- **United Duroc Swine Registry, 1803 W. Detweiller Drive, Peoria, IL 61615. (309) 691-8094**

- **National Spotted Swine Record Association, P.O. Box 249, Bainbridge, IN 46105. (317) 522-6272**

- **Hampshire Swine Registry, 1111 Main Street, Peoria, IL 61606. (309) 674-9134**

- **American Yorkshire Association, 1769 US 52 North, Box 2417, West Lafayette, IN 47906. (317) 463-3593**

Cooperative Extension Information

Kansas State University, Cooperative Extension Service, Manhattan, KA 66506. The following booklets, and others, are available for the asking. Write for a current catalog of offerings.

- **Kansas Swine Nutrition Guide**
- **Kansas Swine Reproduction Guide**

Washington State University Cooperative Extension Service, Department of Agriculture, Pullman, WA 99164. Catalog and price list available for the following literature and more (check your local land-grant university for a similar publication program):

Pork Production Systems with Business Analysis

- **#1036.** *Feeding Purchased Pigs*
- **#1056.** *Producing Feeder Pigs (Low-Investment)*
- **#1162.** *The Low-Investment, Low-Intensity Confinement System (Two groups of Sows, Farrow-to-Finish)*

Management

- **#EB1233.** *Baby Pig Management—Birth to Weaning*
- **#EM4149.** *Care of the Sow during Farrowing and Lactation*

Housing

- **#EM4161.** *Mechanical Ventilation of Swine*
- **#EM4154.** *Swine Confinement Growing-Finishing Units*
- **#EM4163.** *Slotted Floors For Swine*
- **#EM4164.** *Building Materials & Equipment for Swine Facilities*

Nutrition

- **#EB0770.** *Physical Forms of Feed—Feed Processing for Swine*
- **#EB0833.** *Principles of Balancing a Ration*
- **#EB1218.** *Swine Rations*
- **#EM4143.** *Feed Additives for Swine*

Health

- **EB1121.** *Guidelines for the Development of a Swine Herd Health Calendar*
- **#EM4181.** *Infectious Swine Reproductive Diseases*

Waste Management
- #EB1182. *Controlling Odors from Swine Buildings*
- #EM3759. *Animal Manure Data Sheet*
- #EM4165. *Swine Waste Management Alternatives*
- #EM4169. *Flushing Systems for Swine Buildings*
- #EM4483. *Lagoon Systems for Swine Waste Treatment*

Marketing
- #EB0769. *Feeder Pig Marketing Techniques*
- #EB0834. *Choosing a Slaughter Hog Market*

Breeding and Genetics
- #EB1181. *Selection Guidelines for the Seedstock Producer*
- #EB1232. *Crossbreeding Programs for Commercial Pork Production*
- #EM4132. *Boar Selection: Guidelines for Commercial Producers*
- #EM4133. *Guidelines for Choosing Replacement Females*

Reproduction
- #EB0766. *Economics of Reproductive Performance and Breeding Herd Management*
- #1037. *Managing Sows and Gilts During Breeding for Efficient Reproduction*
- #EB1120. *Artificial Insemination in Swine*
- #EM4135. *Management of the Boar*

Miscellaneous
- #PNW75. *Rural Preparedness for Swine Producers*
- #506. *Irrigated Pastures for Hogs*
- #680. *Peas in Swine Rations*
- #0716. *Fat, Cholesterol, and Health*
- #0835. *Recommended Washington Swine Production Practices*
- #EB1073. *Raising Feeder Pigs*
- #EB1113. *How to Produce Biogas from Swine Manure*
- #1179. *1983 Estimated Costs and Returns, 30-Sow Farrow-to-Finish Operation*
- #EM2216. *Swine Improvement & Certification Programs*

Industry Information

Peter Eckrich & Sons, Inc., Consumer Affairs, Box 388, Fort Wayne, IN 46801. This booklet is free for the asking:

- **Meat and You**

Feed Company Literature (check your local feed stores for these and other useful publications):

- **Carnation Company, Swine: A Complete Feeding and Management Program**
- **Cenex, Hog Feeding and Management Guide, Start to Finish**
- **Ralston Purina, Purina Hog Programs**
- **Ralston Purina, High Performance Line From Breeding to Market**
- **Ralston Purina, Purina Welcomes You to the Cage Age**
- **Ralston Purina, Livewire: Sows on Wire**

The Morton Salt Company (P.O. Box 355, Argo, IL 60501), has the following pamphlet available for a large, stamped, self-addressed envelope:

- **A Complete Guide to Home Meat Curing**

The National Pork Producers Council (P.O. Box 10383, Des Moines, IA 50306 (515) 223–2600 or 1776 NW 114th Street, Des Moines, IA 50265 or 499 South Capital Street, SW, Suite #515, Washington, D.C. 20003) can provide insight into pork producer/consumer issues and answers to your meat-related questions.

The Pork Industry Group (PIG) of the National Livestock and Meat Board (444 North Michigan Avenue, Chicago, IL 60611. (312) 467–5520) is probably the very best source of current information on pork consumer issues, including the most recent research findings, recipes, and more. Catalogs and price lists are available for these and other publications (many are free if you only request a single copy):

- **Meat Board Reports (monthly)**
- **Meat Briefings (bi-monthly)**
- **Food & Nutrition News (bi-monthly)**
- **Contribution of Red Meat to the U.S. Diet**
- **Easy Steps: Microwave Cooking with Pork**
- **Exploring the Known: Meat, Diet & Health**
- **The Lean Facts About Pork**
- **Focus on Pork**

- Hog is Man's Best Friend: Meat and By-Products
- Facts About Pork
- Facts About Sausage
- Facts About Ham
- How To Get the Most for Your Pork Dollar
- A Hog's Not All Chops
- The Lean Facts About Pork and Cholesterol
- The Lean Facts About Pork and Calories
- Red Meat in the Diet: A New Look
- Pork on a Budget (recipes)
- Pork's Great Outdoors (recipes)
- Creative Microwaving with Sausage (recipes)
- Calorie Conscious Pork Recipes
- Lard Makes It Better
- Great Ideas for Ground Pork

SUPPLIES

Locate pig-raising supplies such as lumber, fencing, and equipment in your area by visiting several feed suppliers and livestock equipment outlets. You can find addresses and phone numbers in the phone book yellow pages under these listings: Building Materials; Building Materials—Used; Feed Dealers; Fencing; Livestock Dealers; Veterinary Supplies; Lumber—Retail; and others.

The following suppliers advertise in magazines written for pork producers. Write to them for a catalog and current price list.

Fencing and Other Materials

- Bainbridge Enterprises, P.O. Box 52, Marcellus, MI 49067. Fiberglass and plastic hog fencing, custom fit.
- Karsjens Brothers Concrete Products, Inc., Box K-8, Hollandale, MN 56045. Reinforced concrete hog fencing; easily assembled and disassembled to move.
- Long Lasting Farm Equipment, Box 128, Garnavillo, IA 52049. Fourteen-gauge sheet steel for feed and water troughs.

USDA Information

The United States Department of Agriculture (Washington, D.C. 20250) has a 24-hour meat and poultry hotline (202 472–4485) for questions about food safety, preparation, cooking, and related subjects. The following publications are available through the USDA (U.S. Government Printing Office, Washington, D.C. 20402) or your senators and congressmen (all elected officials in Washington, D.C. have lists of publications which they can distribute at no cost to you if you ask). Catalogs of USDA publications are also available. Because some publications are not free, write for current ordering information from the USDA, the U.S. Govt. Printing Office, or your elected officials.

Farmers Bulletins

- #1263. **Breeds of Swine**
- #2224. **Raising Livestock on Small Farms**
- #2240. **Preventing & Controlling Internal Parasites of Hogs**
- #2265. **Pork: Slaughtering, Cutting, Preserving, and Cooking on the Farm**

Home and Garden Bulletins

- # 93. **Freezing Meat and Fish in the Home**
- #106. **Home Canning of Meat and Poultry**
- #160. **Pork in Family Meals: A Guide for Consumers**
- #166. **How to Buy Meat For Your Freezer**

Miscellaneous USDA Publications

- **People on the Farm: Corn and Hog Farming**
- **Crop Reporting Board: Hogs & Pigs**

Appendix D

PRODUCING BIOGAS FROM SWINE MANURE

Swine manure has a potential for energy production, especially on small, remote farms where home-produced energy could be more cost-efficient than the piped-in variety or for large, commercial operations that need to dispose of hundreds of tons of manure at a time. Energy production, can be an extra component in a waste management system.

NATURE'S ENERGY PRODUCING MACHINERY

Methane (CH_4), the major ingredient of natural gas, is an odorless, colorless, flammable gas formed by the decomposition of organic materials in the absence of air. It's been speculated that the natural gas that is piped into our homes for cooking and heating from pockets deep under the earth's crust is the product of organic decay that took place billions of years ago and was subsequently trapped within the earth's layers. Further, it has even been suggested that *sludge* (leftover, undecayed solids) combined with trace gases during methane formation to create, under pressure and over many years of time, what we now call oil.

The methane production process is so simple and so widespread that it still happens. We just never notice it – or its potential as an energy source.

Quite simply, this is how it works: Under anaerobic (without oxygen) conditions, very common acid-forming bacteria digest the carbon contained in organic wastes (such as manure) to form acids and other simpler compounds. When the acid concentration is high enough, methane-forming bacteria digest the acid and release 60 percent methane and 40 percent carbon dioxide, water, and other trace gases. This final byproduct of digestion is called *biogas*.

Natural gas is nearly 100 percent methane. Hence, biogas has a heat value approximately 60 percent of natural gas. Like natural gas, it can be burned for heat and used to power internal combustion engines to generate electricity.

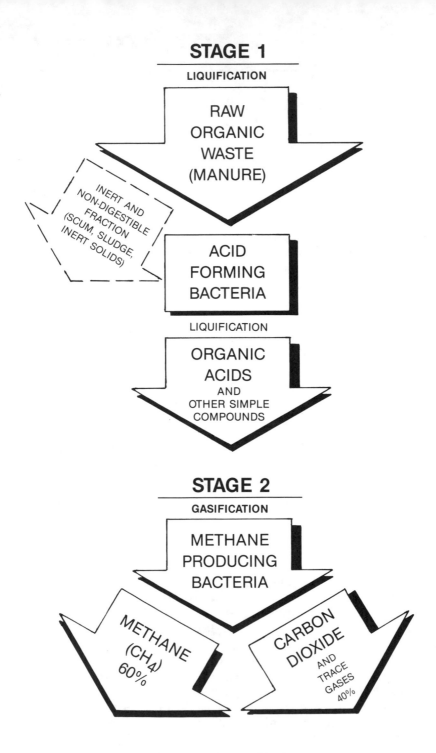

STAGE 1

LIQUIFICATION

RAW
ORGANIC
WASTE
(MANURE)

INERT AND
NON-DIGESTIBLE
FRACTION
(SCUM, SLUDGE,
INERT SOLIDS)

ACID
FORMING
BACTERIA

LIQUIFICATION

ORGANIC
ACIDS
AND
OTHER SIMPLE
COMPOUNDS

STAGE 2

GASIFICATION

METHANE
PRODUCING
BACTERIA

METHANE
(CH_4)
60%

CARBON
DIOXIDE
AND
TRACE
GASES
40%

The stages of anaerobic decay.

At least 9 species of bacteria produce methane gas as a by-product. Many of these are inhabitants of the animal gut. Because the biogas-forming bacteria are so widespread, any time organic material is allowed to decay without air, gas is formed. For instance, sometimes in manure pits below swine confinement buildings and even in garbage dumps covered by soil, the biogas-generation process begins and methane is produced. This unwanted gas can be ignited easily by any stray sparks or even by mixing with oxygen to cause an explosion. Often, if gas formation is a real threat, the excess methane is burned via gas torches, in a process called "flaring off."

BIOGAS PRODUCTION FROM MANURE

The idea of turning animal wastes into usable fuel is not just a far-off dream. In India, where cows outnumber people, methane-generating digesters have been in use on a large scale for many years. Ram Bux Singh, the man behind India's move to biogas, pointed out that the use of cow manure for fuel production was a last chance attempt to provide his country with some of the energy they so desperately need.

Biogas production, while not a difficult process, usually requires a high initial investment in equipment, daily labor, and careful operation for optimum safety and usable gas.

The methane-producing organisms are very sensitive to environmental conditions: Exposure to the air will kill the bacteria — so will antibiotics in the manure; gas production is most rapid between 85 and 105 degrees F. and decreases rapidly below 60 degrees F.; a pH level higher or lower than 6.8 to 8.0 slows gas formation substantially; bacteria function best in 7 to 9 percent solids (about the consistency of cream) with a carbon to nitrogen ratio of 30 to 1. That's a lot of demands that have to be met before the production of burnable gas from manure is possible!

Luckily, the technology to meet the demands of the methane-producing microorganisms is available in the form of an airtight, enclosed tank called a *digester*. It is designed so that it can be filled with raw waste and the spent slurry and gas can be withdrawn easily. Usually, this is accomplished with pipes and pumps.

The digester tank is heavily insulated to conserve the heat generated by the process. If the insulation is not enough to maintain the digester temperature at the optimum 90-95 degrees F., some of the gas is used to heat water which is circulated through the tank via heating coils.

Most animal manures meet the carbon to nitrogen ratio and pH requirements, which is why they are an excellent raw material for fuel production. However, for optimum performance, the bacteria

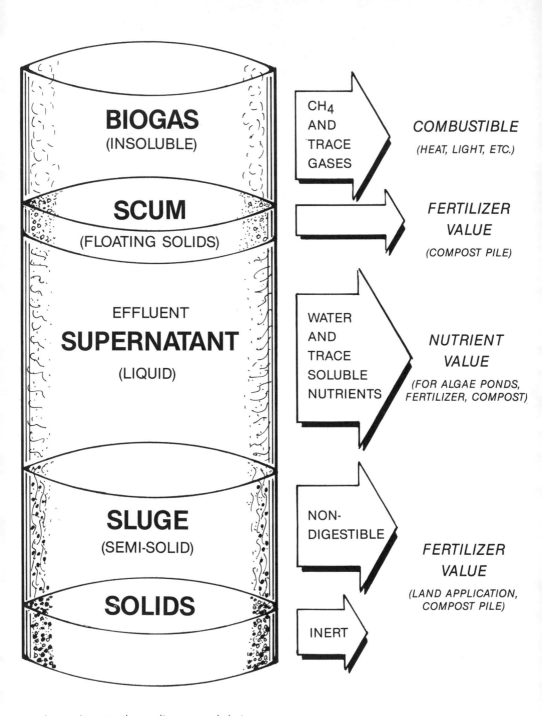

Layers in a methane digester and their uses.

need the manure to be in the form of a *slurry* with 7 to 9 percent solids. Manure collected from under the slotted floors of confinement swine buildings usually contains 3 to 6 percent solids; some of the water must be removed. Flush systems contain even more excess water (0.5 percent solids) and may require a settling basin. Manure scraped from pens is too dense, 10 to 15 percent solids, and will need to have water added.

Agitation (mixing) of the digester slurry is desirable for faster gas production, but it is not essential. If left alone, the digester contents tend to settle into layers.

There are 2 basic ways to operate a digester unit: batch-feeding and continuous-feeding.

Batch-feeding requires only a sporadic input of waste and the digester needs little attention on a daily basis. However, this method requires more labor to load and empty. Further, gas production is inconsistent: it starts slow and then rises to a peak very quickly and finally falls back to zero. However, several batch-fed digesters can assure a continuous gas supply.

Continuous-loading digesters offer a more consistent and rapid rate of gas production by allowing a small, steady quantity of raw material to be piped in daily while sludge and effluent are drawn off. Although this type of system requires little manual labor, it does need almost constant attention to assure that the pumps are working and the pipes do not clog.

The size of the digester is dependent on the type of digester (batch or continuous), the availability of raw materials, the space needed for sludge and effluent to collect, and the amount of gas desired from the digesting unit. Also, digester size is somewhat dependent on the facilities available to pressurize and store the methane.

Swine manure potentially can produce 6 to 8 cubic feet of biogas per pound of total solids (recall that swine waste is 10 to 13 percent solids and is mixed to an 8 percent slurry for digestion), which has the heat value [Btu per cubic foot] of 10 to 12 cubic feet of natural gas.

Finally, the system must include a way to withdraw the biogas from the digester and compress it for storage and use. This requires a gas collection tank sufficient for several days' use, pressure regulators, gauges, relief valves, and gas lines.

The most efficient use of biogas is for the direct heating of barns, out-buildings, and homes; for grain drying, and any other heating or cooking application where the biogas can replace propane or natural gas. When used for heating and cooking, biogas is 75 percent efficient.

To make biogas even more usable and to approach the methane content of natural gas, it must be "scrubbed" to remove the trace gases and water.

The carbon dioxide and ammonia in biogas can be removed by bubbling the gas through limewater. Hydrogen sulfide and other impurities that could corrode pipes, valves, and other equipment are removed by filtering the gas through iron filings (ferric oxide). Finally, the water can be removed by filtering through absorptive chemicals.

Scrubbed biogas is virtually odorless—which could present a problem if you have a leak. Commercial natural gas is given an ingredient to produce its characteristic smell so you know when it is leaking. Not so with pure, home-produced methane. Observe the same cautions as with natural gas use, but especially watch for possible fuel leaks.

If you are interested in more information on this application for your swine manure, we suggest that you find some good book on alternative energy systems (some are listed in Appendix C) and contact your local cooperative extension office for advice and assistance.

BIOGAS APPLICATIONS

Any appliance that runs on natural gas can use pressurized (0.07 to 0.3 pounds per square inch) biogas. Further, many butane and propane appliances also can use this methane-mix fuel. Table D–1 shows some of the potential applications.

Table D–1

RATES OF METHANE USE	
Use	**Rate (cubic feet)**
Cooking	8–16 per hour per small burner
Incubator	0.5–0.7 per hour per cubic foot
Family of five: Cooking & clothes drying, per year	2,000–4,000
Space heating & water, per year (mild climate)	5,000–7,000

Table D–1.

Sources: Davis & Schubert, Alternative Natural Energy Sources In Building Design, 1974, and Leckie, et. al, Other Homes & Garbage, 1975.

Index

Books from

WILLIAMSON PUBLISHING

The Sheep Raiser's Manual
by William Kruesi

"Overall, *The Sheep Raiser's Manual* does a better job of integrating all aspects of sheep farming into a successful sheep enterprise than any other book published in the United States."

Dr. Paul Saenger
New England Farmer

280 pages, 6 × 9, illustrations, photos, charts & graphs.
Quality paperback, $13.95.

Raising Poultry Successfully
by Will Graves

Everything you need to know to raise a small home poultry flock of *chickens, ducks* or *geese* for quality meat or eggs.

196 pages, 6 × 9, illustrations and photos.
Quality paperback, $9.95.

Raising Rabbits Successfully
by Bob Bennett

Written by one of the foremost rabbit authorities, this book is ideal for the beginning rabbit raiser, raising rabbits for food, fun, show and profit.

192 pages, 6 × 9, illustrations and photos.
Quality paperback, $9.95

Home Tanning & Leathercraft Simplified
by Kathy Kellogg

"An exceptionally thorough and readable do-it-yourself book."
Library Journal

192 pages, 6 × 9, step-by-step illustrations, photos, tanning recipes.
Quality paperback, $9.95.

Practical Pole Building Construction
With Plans for Barns, Cabins & Outbuildings
by Leigh Seddon

Complete how-to-build information with original architectural plans for small barn, shed, animal shelter, horse stall, as well as cabins and home.

176 pages, 8½ × 11, over 100 architectural renderings, charts, photos. Quality paperback, $10.95.

Keeping Bees
by John Vivian

Noted homesteader John Vivian packs his book with everything the beekeeper needs to know. Plenty of how-to including building your own hives, stands and feeders.

192 pages, 6 × 9, illustrations and step-by-step photos. Quality paperback, $10.95.

Summer In a Jar: Making Pickles, Jams & More
by Andrea Chesman

Chesman introduces single jar recipes so you can make pickles and relishes a single quart at a time. Plenty of low-sugar jams, marmalades, relishes. Pickles by the crock, too. Outstanding recipes.

160 pages, 8¼ × 7¼, illustrations. Quality paperback, $8.95.

Golde's Homemade Cookies, New Edition
by Golde Hoffman Soloway

Over 100 treasured recipes that defy description. Suffice it to say that no one could walk away from Golde's cookies without asking for another . . . plus the recipe.

160 pages, 8¼ × 7¼, illustrations. Quality paperback, $8.95.

At your bookstore or
To order directly from Williamson Publishing, send check or money order to **Williamson Publishing Co., Church Hill Road, P.O. Box 185, Charlotte, Vermont 05445.**
Please add $2.50 for postage and handling.

Toll-free phone orders with credit cards: 1-800-234-8791.
Satisfaction guaranteed or full refund without questions or quibbles.

37550053
47/70